SHEPHERD'S NOTES

SHEPHERD'S NOTES

When you need a guide through the Scriptures

Haggai/ Malachi

BROADMAN
&HOLMAN
PUBLISHERS

Nashville, Tennessee

Shepherd's Notes®—*Haggai, Zechariah and Malachi*
© 1999
by Broadman & Holman Publishers
Nashville, Tennessee
All rights reserved
Printed in the United States of America

0–8054–9065–5
Dewey Decimal Classification: 224.90
Subject Heading: BIBLE. O.T. HAGGAI
Library of Congress Card Catalog Number: 98–48098

Library of Congress Cataloging-in-Publication Data
Morgan, Barry E.
Haggai, Zechariah & Malachi / Barry Morgan, editor [i.e. author].
    p. cm. — (Shepherd's notes)
    Includes bibliographical references.
    ISBN 0–8054–9065–5 (trade paper)
    1. Bible. O.T. Haggai—Study and teaching.   2. Bible. O.T.
Zechariah—Study and teaching. 3. Bible. O.T. Malachi—Study and teaching.
   I. Title.   II. Title: Haggai, Zechariah, and Malachi.   III. Series
   BS1560.M59   1999
   224'.907—dc21   98–48098
                                           CIP

1 2 3 4 5   03 02 01 00 99

CONTENTS

FOREWORD

Dear Reader:

Shepherd's Notes are designed to give you a quick, step-by-step overview of every book of the Bible. They are not meant to be substitutes for the biblical text; rather, they are study guides intended to help you explore the wisdom of Scripture in personal or group study and to apply that wisdom successfully in your own life.

Shepherd's Notes guide you through the main themes of each book of the Bible and illuminate fascinating details through appropriate commentary and reference notes. Historical and cultural background information brings the Bible into sharper focus.

Six different icons, used throughout the series, call your attention to historical-cultural information, Old Testament and New Testament references, word pictures, unit summaries, and personal application for everyday life.

Whether you are a novice or a veteran at Bible study, I believe you will find *Shepherd's Notes* a resource that will take you to a new level in your mining and applying the riches of Scripture.

In Him,

David R. Shepherd
Editor-in-Chief

DESIGNED FOR THE BUSY USER

Shepherd's Notes for Haggai, Zechariah, and Malachi is designed to provide an easy-to-use tool for getting a quick handle on these significant Bible books' important features, and for gaining an understanding of their messages. Information available in more difficult-to-use reference works has been incorporated into the *Shepherd's Notes* format. This brings you the benefits of many advanced and expensive works packed into one small volume.

Shepherd's Notes are for laymen, pastors, teachers, small-group leaders and participants, as well as the classroom student. Enrich your personal study or quiet time. Shorten your class or small-group preparation time as you gain valuable insights into the truths of God's Word that you can pass along to your students or group members.

DESIGNED FOR QUICK ACCESS

Bible students with time constraints will especially appreciate the timesaving features built into the *Shepherd's Notes*. All features are intended to aid a quick and concise encounter with the heart of the messages of Haggai, Zechariah, and Malachi.

Concise Commentary. Short sections provide quick "snapshots" of the themes of these books, highlighting important points and other information.

Outlined Text. Comprehensive outlines cover the entire text of Haggai, Zechariah, and Malachi. This is a valuable feature for following each book's flow, allowing for a quick, easy way to locate a particular passage.

Shepherd's Notes. These summary statements or capsule thoughts appear at the close of every key section of the narratives. While functioning in part as a quick summary, they also deliver the essence of the message presented in the sections which they cover.

Icons. Various icons in the margin highlight recurring themes in the books of Haggai, Zechariah, and Malachi, aiding in selective searching or tracing of those themes.

Sidebars and Charts. These specially selected features provide additional background information to your study or preparation. Charts offer a quick overview of important subjects. Sidebars include definitions as well as cultural, historical, and biblical insights.

Questions to Guide Your Study. These thought-provoking questions and discussion starters are designed to encourage interaction with the truth and principles of God's Word.

DESIGNED TO WORK FOR YOU

Personal Study. Using the *Shepherd's Notes* with a passage of Scripture can enlighten your study and take it to a new level. At your fingertips is information that would require searching several volumes to find. In addition, many points of application occur throughout the volume, contributing to personal growth.

Teaching. Outlines frame the text of Haggai, Zechariah, and Malachi, providing a logical presentation of their messages. Capsule thoughts designated as "Shepherd's Notes" provide summary statements for presenting the essence of key points and events. Application icons point out personal application of the messages of the books. Historical Context icons indicate where cultural and historical background information is supplied.

Group Study. *Shepherd's Notes* can be an excellent companion volume to use for gaining a quick but accurate understanding of the messages of Haggai, Zechariah, and Malachi. Each group member can benefit from having his or her own copy. The *Note's* format accommodates the study of themes throughout Haggai, Zechariah, and Malachi. Leaders may use its flexible features to prepare for group sessions or use them during group sessions. Questions to guide your study can spark discussion of Haggai, Zechariah, and Malachi's key points and truths to be discovered in these profound books.

LIST OF MARGIN ICONS USED IN HAGGAI, ZECHARIAH, AND MALACHI

Shepherd's Notes. Placed at the end of each section, a capsule statement provides the reader with the essence of the message of that section.

Historical Context. To indicate historical information—historical, biographical, cultural—and provide insight on the understanding or interpretation of a passage.

Old Testament Reference. Used when the writer refers to Old Testament passages or when Old Testament passages illuminate a text.

New Testament Reference. Used when the writer refers to New Testament passages that are either fulfilled prophecy, an antitype of an Old Testament type, or a New Testament text which in some other way illuminates the passages under discussion.

Personal Application. Used when the text provides a personal or universal application of truth.

Word Picture. Indicates that the meaning of a specific word or phrase is illustrated so as to shed light on it.

HAGGAI

INTRODUCTION

Haggai is one of the prophetic books of the Old Testament included among the minor prophets. The book received its name from the prophet who delivered the word of the Lord. Haggai was the first prophet to arise among the Jewish people following their return from the Babylonian Exile.

Haggai's name may be derived from the Hebrew word for "festival." Nothing more than the prophet's name is known from the Bible.

Jeremiah specifically prophesied the destruction of Jerusalem, the Temple, and the seventy-year exile. Jeremiah also foretold the return of the inhabitants of Judah to their homeland at the end of the seventy-year period (see Jer. 25.11–12). Jeremiah reported that the Babylonians burned the Temple, destroyed the city of Jerusalem, and carried many of the inhabitants into exile on the tenth day of the fifth month in the nineteenth year of King Nebuchadnezzar (586 B.C.) (see Jer. 52:12–15).

To understand the book of Haggai, we must appreciate its historical background. In 586 B.C. the city of Jerusalem was captured by the Babylonians under the leadership of King Nebuchadnezzar. The city was devastated and the Temple built by Solomon was destroyed. As was typical following the conquest of an enemy nation, the Babylonians deported a large portion of the population of Judah into exile, where they remained for approximately seventy years.

In 539 B.C. the Persians conquered the Babylonian Empire. A year later the Persian king, Cyrus the Great, issued a decree granting permission

1

for the exiled inhabitants of Judah to return to their homeland and to rebuild their Temple.

The decree issued by Cyrus in 538 B.C. to rebuild Jerusalem and the Temple was foretold by the prophet Isaiah approximately one hundred and fifty years earlier (Isa. 44:28). Approximately fifty thousand Jewish people, led by Zerubbabel and Joshua, made the trek back to Judah, arriving around 536 B.C. According to reports contained in the book of Ezra, the altar of the Temple was rebuilt and burnt offerings once again presented to the Lord in the seventh month of the year. The foundation of the Temple was completed in the second month of the second year after the exiles returned (see Ezra 3:1–10). Construction on the Temple, however, then ceased.

Conditions in the land of Judah were difficult. The returning exiles had to begin from scratch to rebuild their lives as families and as a people. The initial enthusiasm to rebuild the city of Jerusalem and its Temple gave way to discouragement and apathy as the struggle to provide the necessities of life became the prime focus of the people. Consequently, work on the Temple ceased and did not resume until the second year of the reign of the Persian king Darius, 520 B.C. The reconstruction was renewed in response to the prophetic ministries of Haggai and Zechariah (see Ezra 4:24–5:2).

In addition to the struggle to provide for daily needs, the inhabitants of Jerusalem faced opposition from the Samaritans. When the exiles returned to Judah, the Samaritans had initially requested to help rebuild the Temple. Although the Samaritans were distantly related to the

The books of Ezra and Nehemiah provide information helpful to keep in mind when studying the book of Haggai. Although Ezra and Nehemiah lived and worked in Jerusalem subsequent to the ministry of Haggai, the books bearing their names describe events contemporary with the day of Haggai. In fact, Ezra explicitly mentioned the ministries of Haggai and Zechariah and the results of their prophetic labors (Ezra 5:1; 6:14).

inhabitants of Judah, the returning exiles regarded the Samaritans as violators of the Mosaic Law. The Samaritans had married people who worshiped gods other than God who had made a covenant with Israel. (For more information on the Samaritans, see the article in the *Holman Bible Dictionary*.)

When the leaders of Judah rejected the request by the Samaritans to help reconstruct the Temple, the Samaritans tried to disrupt and to prevent work on the Temple and the city of Jerusalem. This opposition by the Samaritans and the resulting discouragement was a factor in stopping the reconstruction of the Temple (see Ezra 4:1–5).

INTRODUCTION TO THE FIRST MESSAGE (1:1–2)

Haggai seemed particularly concerned to provide specific chronological information concerning the time of his prophetic ministry (see 1:1, 15; 2:1, 10, 18, 20). This chronological attention, extending even to the precise days when Haggai received messages from the Lord, indicates that this prophetic book is associated closely with the historical realities existing in the time of the prophet.

Haggai received his first message from the Lord on the first day of the sixth month in the second year of King Darius—that is, in the month of Elul (August-September) of the year 520 B.C.

This was the Persian king, Darius I Hystaspes, who reigned from 521 to 486 B.C.

The first word of the Lord which came to Haggai was to be delivered to Zerubbabel, the civil leader of the inhabitants of Judah, and to Joshua, the religious leader of Judah. Zerubbabel, the

Haggai was not just providing challenging sermons for the inhabitants of Judah. He was speaking to specific conditions and situations which existed in his society and culture. What about our teaching, preaching, and study? Do we follow the prophetic pattern? Do we seek to hear God's message in the context of life as we experience it?

According to 1 Chronicles 3:17–19, Zerubbabel was the son of Pedaiah, the brother of Shealtiel. Both Matthew and Luke, however, in their genealogies of Jesus agree that Zerubbabel was a son of Shealtiel (see Matt. 1:12; Luke 3:27). Some scholars have sought to sort this out by suggesting that Zerubbabel was a son of Shealtiel as the result of a levirate marriage (Deut. 25:5–10) between Shealtiel's childless widow and his brother Pedaiah. The son produced by this union, Zerubbabel, would, therefore, legally be regarded as the son of Shealtiel.

son of Shealtiel, a descendant of King David (1 Chron. 3:17–19; Matt. 1:12; Luke 3:27), was appointed governor of the land of Judah by the Persian king. Both Zerubbabel and Joshua had been instrumental in leading the exiles back to their homeland following the decree of Cyrus the Great in 538 B.C. (see Ezra 1–2, where Joshua apparently is referred to as Jeshua; Ezra 2:2). They had guided the inhabitants of Judah in rebuilding the altar for the Temple and laying the Temple's foundation (Ezra 3:2, 8–10).

As the recognized leaders of the people of Judah, Zerubbabel and Joshua had the responsibility to guide God's people to follow His will. God sent Haggai to speak to these two men. It was their responsibility as leaders to influence the people to obey the word of God through His prophet.

God expressed displeasure with a widespread attitude in Judah. The people were concentrating on building their own homes and taking care of their own needs exclusively. As far as they were concerned, the construction of God's house would have to wait until they had completed their own houses and had taken care of their own needs.

How many times in our own lives today do we postpone and delay obedience to God's directions because it seems to be an inconvenient time or because we are too busy with more pressing matters? Does God not realize that we have urgent tasks on our to-do lists? The truth of the matter is that often our priorities are not God's priorities. As the book of Haggai will demonstrate, until God's priorities become our priorities, all of our efforts and labors will be far less

The designation "Lord of hosts" occurs in Haggai fourteen times. Zechariah uses it fifty-three times, and Malachi, twenty-four times. Scholars have disagreed concerning the precise meaning of the term "hosts." The term has been alleged to refer to "stars" or to "angels" or to "the armies of Israel." Despite the lack of agreement on the meaning of "hosts," the significance of this designation for God is to emphasize His greatness and power.

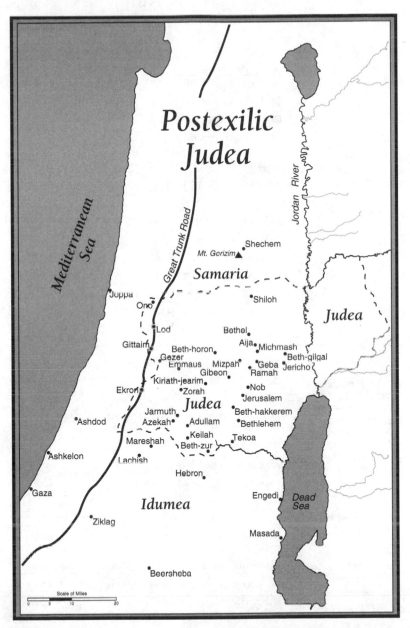

Taken from, Mervin Breneman, *Ezra, Nehemiah, Esther,* vol. 10, New American Commentary (Nashville, Tenn.: Broadman & Holman Publishers, 1993), p. 13.

productive than they would have been if we had been obedient to God's directions and priorities.

- *Although addressed specifically to Zerubba-*
- *bel and Joshua, God's message indicted the*
- *inhabitants of Judah for their self-seeking,*
- *self-interested priorities.*

FIRST MESSAGE: CONSIDER YOUR WAYS (1:3–11)

A Challenging Question and a Critical Exhortation (1:3–7)

After addressing Zerubbabel and Joshua concerning the attitude of the people toward the reconstruction of the Temple, Haggai delivered God's message to the people themselves. He began with a challenging and convicting question. The people had concluded that the time was not right to rebuild the house of God. God now wanted to know if the time was right for them to build themselves paneled houses while His own house remained in ruins.

The reference to "paneled houses" implied luxurious dwellings, not just simple homes. In other words, not only were the people refusing to accept God's priorities as their priorities; they were also pursuing their own priorities to a self-indulgent, self-gratifying extreme. They were not content with adequate, comfortable homes; they wanted luxurious "paneled houses."

After asking a question designed to challenge and to convict His people, God issued a critical exhortation. In fact, God twice exhorted His people to consider their ways (1:5, 7). He instructed His people to examine their lives and to reflect on what had been occurring to them.

Life had been difficult and not too prosperous or successful. God wanted His people to consider the reason why their lives had met with such little blessing. Although they were diligently working and attempting to make a living, no matter how much energy they invested or how much they labored, they just could not seem to keep up—let alone get ahead.

After reminding His people of the rather dismal quality of their lives, God repeated His initial exhortation: "Consider your ways!" (1:7). It is as if God said to His people, "This is what is taking place in your lives. Think about it! Why is this happening?"

God sometimes uses the events in our lives to get our attention. Sometimes unpleasant events are the result of disobedience to God. We should not conclude, however, that unpleasant events are always the result of sin and disobedience in our lives. The book of Job reminds us that occasionally those with whom God is pleased, those whose lives are lived in obedience to His will, may encounter suffering and disaster. The life of Jesus, of course, is the supreme example of this fact.

Does our obedience to the Lord sometimes take a backseat to "keeping up with the Joneses"? Is our attitude often one that demonstrates that indulging our own desires and fancies comes before serving the Lord? Do we seek God's kingdom and His righteousness first (Matt. 6:33), or do we plan to do so just as soon as we get our important projects and goals accomplished?

- Through a probing question and a
- twice-repeated exhortation, God instructed
- His people to evaluate their lives and their
- conduct.

God's Explanation of Current Events (1:8–11)

Before explaining why His people were experiencing what they were experiencing in their daily lives, God issued a command. He instructed them to gather the necessary materials and to complete the reconstruction of His Temple. God further informed His people that they were to do this so He might be pleased and glorified.

After exhorting His people to reflect upon their lives, God then explained the reason for their difficulties. As God's chosen people, they had good reason to expect much from life, and they did. Unfortunately, their experiences did not match their expectations. Why? God explained the reason: they had their priorities wrong. As a consequence, God informed them that He had withheld blessings and prosperity from their lives. God did not hesitate to take responsibility for the difficult conditions which His people were experiencing. The drought and the lack of productivity were due to the people's lack of obedience, but God was the One who sent the drought and lack of productivity. Clearly, this was one of the times when unpleasant and difficult conditions were due to sin.

To please and to glorify God should be the motivation for all that we do. Paul commanded, "Whatever you do, do it all for the glory of God" (1 Cor. 10:31).

■ *God explained to His people that He had*
■ *withheld the expected blessings and prosper-*
■ *ity because in a spirit of disobedience they*
■ *had ceased to rebuild the Temple.*

RESPONSE TO THE FIRST MESSAGE (1:12–15)

Haggai's first message met with success. The primary recipients of the message, Zerubbabel and Joshua, responded favorably to the word of the Lord. Many others also responded in obedience to and reverence for the Lord.

The response of Zerubbabel, Joshua, and the remnant of the people to the message delivered by Haggai indicates that they had heard the Lord. To hear the Lord means we obey what we have heard.

The original language literally says that the people "feared before the Lord" (1:12). The fear involved here was not that of cowering fright due to the presence of a cruel, sadistic despot. Rather, this fear was an accurate and appropriate appreciation of the power, majesty, holiness, and glory of God

Once His people responded with obedience and reverence, God sent Haggai with a word of encouragement. Life itself had not suddenly become easier or more pleasant. All of the difficulties still existed. The enemies were just as virulent in their opposition. The task was just as imposing. And the people's spirits were just as low. Consequently, they needed assurance that they were not undertaking the reconstruction of the Temple alone. God sent Haggai to encourage the people with the promise of His presence. For God to promise His presence, of course, did not mean that He was simply an interested spectator to the reconstruction. For God to promise "I am with you" meant that He was present to help, to equip, to enable, and to protect.

God's presence with His people manifested itself in the equipping of the people to do what He had commanded them to do. God stirred up the spirits of Zerubbabel, Joshua, and the people so that they resumed the work on the Temple. To stir up their spirits suggests that God placed in His people a zeal for the work and a commitment to accomplish it.

To launch out in obedience to what God has said to do is the first step in experiencing God's power and enablement. To wait until we feel like we have received the power and enablement is often an act of disobedience that dissuades God from stirring up our spirits.

Haggai reported that the good intentions of the people were translated into actual obedience. The rebuilding of the Temple was resumed approximately three weeks after Haggai had delivered the initial message from the Lord.

The second year of Darius the king would have been 520 B.C. The second month would have been the Jewish month of Elul (August-September).

■ *In response to His people's obedience and*
■ *reverence for Him, God promised His pres-*
■ *ence and His power to enable them to accom-*
■ *plish the task which He had commanded.*

QUESTIONS TO GUIDE YOUR STUDY

1. When God exhorted His people to "consider their ways," what did He intend for them to realize? (1:3–7)
2. Why were the inhabitants of Judah experiencing such difficult and discouraging conditions in their lives? (1:9–11)
3. Which came first—the people's commitment to obey God and to reverence Him through rebuilding the Temple, or God's encouragement to them concerning the rebuilding project? (1:12–15)

SECOND MESSAGE: TAKE COURAGE AND BUILD (2:1–9)

Once again Haggai provided a precise chronological marker for his message. Almost a month after the construction of the Temple had resumed, God sent Haggai with another message for His people.

The timing of this second message may be significant. The Day of Atonement was a recent memory. The Feast of Booths (also known as the Feast of Tabernacles) was just concluding. Many people had visited the Temple to participate in these religious observances. As they took part in the ceremonies in the Temple precincts, they may well have taken note of how much work remained and how shabby the Temple looked in comparison to its former glory. This would have been particularly true if some of the worshipers had visited the original Temple prior to its destruction. God sent Haggai in the month of Tishri with a word of encouragement in response to the dejection which He observed in His people as they worshiped in a Temple that seemed to hold little promise for the future.

Initially Haggai was sent to the leaders, Zerubbabel and Joshua. On the occasion of this second message, Haggai was directed to speak not only to Zerubbabel and Joshua but also to the remnant of the people as well. The leaders had accepted their responsibilities to lead the people to follow God's will. The people had accepted their responsibility to be obedient to God's will. Now God had a message for the leaders and the people alike.

The second message began with three questions posed by God to the recipients (2:3). These questions implied that the people were becoming disillusioned and discouraged as they compared the Temple on which they were working to the glorious Temple that had been constructed by Solomon and destroyed by the Babylonians. Among the returned exiles there may have been some who had seen the first Temple in its glory. Their comparisons may have served to dishearten the younger generation at work in the rebuilding. Therefore, the Lord had a special word of encouragement to deliver through Haggai. God exhorted the recipients to take courage because His presence was with them. This is the second occurrence of this statement in the book of Haggai (see 1:13).

Because God was present in their midst, because His presence indicated His blessings and enablement, because His presence suggested His favor and commitment, the people

The month Tishri was a significant month in the religious calendar of the Jewish people. The first day of Tishri was *Rosh Hashanah*, the Jewish new year; the tenth day of Tishri was *Yom Kippur*, the Day of Atonement; and the fifteenth day of Tishri marked the beginning of the seven-day-long observance of the Feast of Tabernacles. The Feast of Tabernacles was one of the three annual festivals when Jewish males were required to visit the Temple in Jerusalem (Exod. 34:23; Deut. 16:16).

How many times have we become discouraged when we have compared our labors to that of someone else? How often has our commitment lagged when we felt that what we had to offer could not measure up to the achievements of others? Perhaps we, too, need to take courage and work, trusting that God is with us and that what He wants is our obedience.

The apostle Paul expressed a similar sentiment in his letter to the Romans. Paul asked his recipients, "If God is for us, who can be against us?" (Rom. 8:31).

should take courage and continue the work. Even if the present Temple paled in comparison to the former Temple, there was no cause for despair and lack of enthusiasm. God was with them; they were acting in obedience to Him; therefore, they must not lose spirit and become discouraged.

In order to reinforce the assurance of His presence with His people, God reminded them of the commitment He made when He led them out of Egypt under the leadership of Moses. According to the book of Exodus, God specifically promised to dwell among the sons of Israel and to be their God (Exod. 29:45–46). Furthermore, He promised His presence to go with the Israelites as they journeyed to the Promised Land (Exod. 33:14). In a similar fashion, God promised the people in the day of Haggai that His Spirit was abiding in their midst. If God's Spirit was abiding in their midst, then what did they have to fear?

As the discouraged and disillusioned workers compared the results of their labors to the previous Temple, they probably considered their resources to be too meager to adorn the Temple with the costly and beautiful furnishings that were a part of Solomon's Temple. Consequently, God issued a promise that should have encouraged them in their efforts. He promised that in a little while He would shake the heavens and the earth, the sea, the dry land, and the nations (2:6). As a result of this shaking, the nations would come to the Temple bringing their wealth; and God would fill His Temple with glory (2:7). In fact, to assure His people that He could and would accomplish these feats, God announced that the silver and gold belonged to Him. Although nations and peoples might believe that they possessed great wealth and riches, God confirmed that their possessions ultimately belonged to Him.

The author of the book of Hebrews (12:18–29) referred to Haggai 2:6–7 in at least two ways. First of all, he saw the passage in Haggai as a historical reference to the giving of the Law at Mount Sinai (Heb. 12:18–21; see also Exod. 19:7–25). Secondly, the author of Hebrews used Haggai 2:6 to refer to a future, eschatological shaking of the earth and the heavens (Heb. 12:26–27). The created order will be shaken so that only those things which cannot be shaken will remain. This language should probably call to mind the judgment of God at the end of the age when the present created order will be destroyed and the new heaven and the new earth instituted (see 2 Pet. 3:10–13).

God informed the inhabitants of Judah that He would once again shake the created order. When did the first shaking occur? Based upon Hebrews 12:18–21, the initial shaking may refer to the giving of the Law at Mount Sinai. The second shaking may be a reference to the judgment of God in the last day (see Heb. 12:26–27). This does not preclude the possibility of partial fulfillments prior to the ultimate fulfillment. Many scholars, for example, see partial fulfillments in Jesus, one greater than the Temple coming to Jerusalem (Matt. 12:6), or in the lavish provision for the Temple by King Artaxerxes I of Persia during the ministry of Ezra (see Ezra 7:11–24). Other scholars suggest that at least a partial fulfillment may also be seen in the refurbishing and beautification project of the Temple which Herod the Great undertook beginning in 20 B.C.

Herod the Great (37 B.C.–4 B.C.), an Idumean, was reigning as king of the Jewish people at the time of Jesus' birth. Although he was never accepted by the Jewish people, Herod did undertake lavish improvements upon the structure of the Jewish Temple in Jerusalem. As a result of the efforts of Herod the Great, the Temple in Jerusalem was regarded as one of the most beautiful structures of the day (see Mark 13:1). For additional information concerning the rebuilding and beautification project initiated by Herod, see the article, "Temple of Jerusalem," in the *Holman Bible Dictionary*.

How often do we regard our daily work to be merely mundane, unimpressive labor? Do we lose sight of the fact that God can take our faithful labor, no matter how commonplace or even tedious it may seem, and use it to achieve His purposes? What might God want to accomplish through our faithful labor today?

■ Although God's people became discouraged
■ as they worked on the Temple, God encour-
■ aged them and promised peace and glory in
■ the future for His house. He reminded His
■ people that He was the One who owned all
■ the riches of the world and that, through His
■ Spirit, He was abiding in their midst. Conse-
■ quently, they possessed all the resources they
■ could possibly need.

THIRD MESSAGE: CONSIDER THE PAST; COMMIT TO THE FUTURE (2:10–19)

Just a little over two months after the previous message (2:1), and exactly three months after the construction on the Temple had resumed (1:15), God sent Haggai to deliver the third message. The twenty-fourth day of the ninth month, the Jewish month of Chislev, corresponds to our months of November-December.

This third message took an approach different from the previous two. This time God called for a ruling from the priests concerning some legal matters pertaining to religious rituals and ceremonial contamination. Haggai was instructed to gather the priests and to ask them to render a legal decision with regard to two situations.

The first situation involved carrying holy meat in the fold of a garment. "Holy meat" referred to meat that had been dedicated to God and presented to Him in the form of one of the sacrifices. Haggai asked the priests whether this holy meat could convey holiness to other items with which it might come in contact. The priests answered correctly by responding negatively.

Next Haggai presented the situation of ritual contamination involving someone who had touched a deceased person. To touch a corpse was considered one of the most serious defilements possible. Such defilement lasted seven days and could only be removed by twice purifying the body with the ashes of the red heifer (Num. 19).

Haggai asked the priests to render a verdict: if a person who had touched a corpse, and thus became unclean, should touch cooked food, wine, oil, or any other food, would that which was touched become unclean also? The priests answered correctly that ritual contamination would be imparted to the items. The apparent lesson seemed clear: While holiness cannot be spread through contact with the holy, uncleanness can be communicated through contact with the unclean.

The apostle Paul applied this asymmetrical principle of holiness and uncleanness to personal conduct. According to 1 Corinthians 15:33, "bad company corrupts good character." Hasn't it often been our experience that one "bad apple" will spoil the whole bushel? One of the facts of life is that evil frequently seems to be much more pervasive and contagious than goodness and holiness. It still seems to be the case that holiness cannot be easily communicated, whereas uncleanness and unrighteousness will be spread vigorously through contact

The regulations concerning the offering of the red heifer and the purification ceremony for one who had touched a corpse are described in Numbers 19. If these purifications were not performed on the specified days, the person was not considered clean; and he was to be cut off from Israel—he was excluded from his nation or perhaps even executed (see Exod. 31:14; Lev. 20:2–5; Num. 15:30). The person who had been defiled by touching a corpse would then defile anything or anyone else whom he touched (Num. 19:22).

with that which is morally impure and unwholesome in our lives.

Lest there be any doubt concerning the point of the questions which he had asked, Haggai made specific application to his countrymen. In doing so, Haggai reminded the people of the conditions which existed prior to their recommitment to the construction of the Temple. According to Haggai, God considered His people, and everything they did, to be unclean. Even what they offered to God was considered by Him to be unclean. The connection to the questions posed by Haggai seems to be that even though God's holy Temple was in the midst of this people, that did not make the people themselves holy. Holiness could not be communicated through mere contact with the holy. On the other hand, the people were unclean in that they had chosen their own ways, their own priorities, and their own wills instead of God's. They were unclean; and, consequently, everything which they touched became defiled.

Already God had twice instructed the people to consider their ways (1:5, 7). Now He instructed them twice more to consider what was taking place (2:15, 18). They needed to pay attention to what had taken place in their recent past and the reasons for it (2:15–17). They also needed to consider what God had in store for them in the future (2:18–19).

God reminded the inhabitants of Judah of the lack of productivity of the land during the period when they had ceased to work on the Temple (2:15–17). What had occurred had not happened by chance or coincidence. Rather, God Himself had caused the diminished harvests, the destruction of the produce by wind, hail, and mildew for a specific purpose: He was intervening in the lives of His people to cause them to turn to Him (2:17). Unfortunately, His people had not responded by turning back to the Lord. They had continued to complain about the lack of success of their labors, the harshness of their existence, and the "unfortunate" events that seemed continually to hinder them from achieving the success and prosperity they sought.

God reminded His people of their recent past in order to speak to them concerning their future. "The day when the temple of the LORD was founded" (2:18, NASB) might refer to the erection of the altar and the initial laying of the foundation of the Temple when the exiles had returned from the Babylonian Exile (see Ezra 3.10). On the other hand, the reference might be to the resumption of the work after almost sixteen years of inactivity (Hag. 1:14–15). Regardless of which starting point is used for the reference, the message remains the same. Until the people responded in obedience, as was the case on the twenty-fourth of the ninth month (2:10, 18), to make God's priority their priority and to complete the construction of the Temple, they had experienced unproductive crops and a struggle for existence.

Now God invited them to consider what He would do from this day forward. Due to their obedience in engaging in the rebuilding of His house, God promised to bless His people. His blessings had been withheld due to their disobedience, but now His blessings would be unleashed upon them for their obedience.

The Bible clearly and repeatedly teaches that God does bless His people for their obedience. We need to be careful, however, not to make two mistakes in regard to this teaching. First, the motivation of our obedience should not be the blessings we may receive but our love for God and our desire that He be glorified. Second, we should not think that God's blessings are only measured by prosperity, health, and pleasant circumstances in our lives.

S N

■ *God reminded His people that the past diffi-*
■ *culties which they had experienced were due*
■ *to their lack of obedience. Their present obe-*
■ *dience insured that He would bless them and*
■ *their efforts.*

FOURTH MESSAGE: AN EXALTED FUTURE FOR ZERUBBABEL (2:20–23)

For the second time in the same day Haggai received a message from the Lord. This message differed from the previous ones, however, in that it was specifically addressed to Zerubbabel alone. God had a word of encouragement for this leader of the people.

In this fourth message, God spoke directly to Zerubbabel to encourage him and to make a promise concerning his destiny. God referred to a future day when He would shake the heavens and the earth and would overthrow kingdoms and powers (see 2:6–7, where similar language was used). The terminology suggests that God was referring to a future triumph and victory over hostile powers and kingdoms. God informed Zerubbabel that the victory would be accomplished by God Himself.

Although God did not specifically mention anyone or any people as His instrument to accomplish this victory, we should not rule out the possibility of God using a servant of His choosing to achieve this victory. In the Old Testament, God frequently promised that He would accomplish a victory, and then He used the armies of Israel to win the battle (see, for example, Deut. 7:1–2). Of course, there were other times when God commanded Israel to stand still and watch the victory which He would accomplish without their involvement (see, for example, 2 Chron. 20:15–17).

God promised Zerubbabel that on the day that He shook the heavens and the earth and procured the victory over the kingdoms of the nations, He would make Zerubbabel, His servant, like a signet ring. Through the use of this terminology, God, therefore, may have intended for Zerubbabel to understand that he would be precious to the Lord and that God would never cast him aside.

Haggai's reference to Zerubbabel as God's signet ring has an interesting background. Jeremiah had informed Jehoiachin (also known as Coniah or Jeconiah), the king of Judah (597 B.C.), that even though he were a signet ring on the right hand of God, God would pull him off and give him into the hand of Nebuchadnezzar, king of Babylon (Jer. 22:24–25). Haggai, speaking seventy-seven years later, took up this same terminology and reversed it when speaking to Zerubbabel, a grandson of Jehoiachin (see 1 Chron. 3:16–19).

Since Zerubbabel was a descendant of David, the language in this promise may be a reminder that God had chosen the lineage of David to bring about His Servant, the Messiah (see 2 Sam. 7:8–16). Although Zerubbabel was a vassal governor under the Persian Empire and prospects for the Davidic kingdom did not appear very bright, God promised that there would be a triumphal day in the future when the lineage which Zerubbabel represented would participate in the glorious victory accomplished by God. The promise made to Zerubbabel, therefore, was a messianic promise

A signet ring was a cherished and valuable possession of an ancient monarch. This ring was the seal by which the king authenticated some possession to belong to him, to be genuine, and to be under his protection. Consequently, a signet ring was a possession which the monarch held dear and with which he was not likely to part.

Of course, this promise to Zerubbabel was ultimately fulfilled in Jesus Christ, the son of David and descendent of Zerubbabel (Matt. 1:12; Luke 3:27). Jesus has received the throne of His father David and His kingdom will have no end (Luke 1:32–33). Furthermore, the kingdom inaugurated by Jesus will one day be victorious over all hostile powers and kingdoms (1 Cor. 15:23–28, 57).

indicating that Zerubbabel was God's chosen servant through whom the promises made to David would ultimately be fulfilled. Like a valued and cherished signet ring, Zerubbabel and his descendants would never be cast off by the King of heaven and earth.

- *The last message delivered by Haggai was*
- *addressed to Zerubbabel and promised a des-*
- *tiny and victory to him which were ulti-*
- *mately fulfilled in his descendant, the*
- *Messiah, Jesus Christ.*

QUESTIONS TO GUIDE YOUR STUDY

1. Does God need our money and our wealth in order to accomplish His plans for the world? (2:8)
2. Why did the people rebuilding the Temple become discouraged as the project progressed? (2:1–9)
3. Does God's sovereign involvement in His people's lives extend only to what are usually considered the major issues, or does it extend even to the minute details of everyday living? (2:15–19)

INTRODUCTION

Zechariah is one of the prophetic books included among the minor prophets. As one of the post-exilic prophets, Zechariah was a contemporary of the prophet Haggai. Post-exilic prophets ministered to the Jewish people after they had returned to the land of Judah following the Babylonian Exile (see the historical background comments in the discussion of Haggai). To understand the historical context for the book of Zechariah, one should read the Old Testament books of Ezra, Nehemiah, and Haggai (see the corresponding volume, *Shepherd's Notes: Ezra and Nehemiah*).

Zechariah identified himself as the son of Berechiah, the son of Iddo (in Ezra 5:1 and 6:14, however, he is designated the son of Iddo). Since Zechariah's grandfather, Iddo, was head of one of the priestly families which returned from exile under the leadership of Zerubbabel and Joshua (Neh. 12:4), we know that Zechariah was of priestly descent. In fact, he succeeded his grandfather as head of the priestly family during the high priesthood of Joiakim (also known as Jehoiakim, Neh 12:16). Zechariah probably was quite a young man when the exiles returned from Babylonia after the decree of Cyrus the Great, king of Persia, in 538 B.C. The fact that he is referred to as "that young man" (Zech. 2:4), suggests that he was still a young man at the time of his prophetic ministry.

Like Haggai, Zechariah was commissioned to his prophetic ministry to exhort the people of Judah to resume the construction on the Temple in Jerusalem (see Ezra 5:1; 6:14).

Zechariah, a frequently occurring name in the Old Testament, means "he whom God remembers."

Haggai began his ministry in the sixth month, Elul (August-September), of the second year of Darius I Hystaspes, i.e., 520 B.C. (Hag. 1:1).

Zechariah first prophesied in the eighth month, Marcheshvan (October-November) (Zech. 1:1), two months after Haggai began his prophetic work. The prophetic labors of Haggai and Zechariah were successful; the people resumed the construction of the Temple in the month of Elul, 520 B.C., and completed the work in the month of Adar (February-March), 516 B.C. (see Hag. 1:15; Ezra 6:15). No one knows how long the ministry of Zechariah lasted. It entailed at least three years (see the reference to the fourth year of Darius in 7:1), but how much beyond the year 518 B.C. Zechariah ministered cannot be determined with certainty.

The book of Zechariah is the longest in the collection of the minor prophets. The first eight chapters contain accounts of visions which Zechariah received. Chapters 9 to 14, on the other hand, have a markedly different format. Instead of visions, they record prophetic messages directed toward two different nations, the land of Hadrach (9:1) and the land of Israel (12:1).

FIRST MESSAGE: A CALL FOR REPENTANCE (1:1–6)

The book of Zechariah begins with an introduction of the prophet himself and a chronological reference indicating the beginning of his ministry (1:1) in 520 B.C. Darius was Darius I Hystaspes, the king of Persia, who reigned from 521 B.C. to 486 B.C. Zechariah characterized the message which he delivered as "the word of the Lord [which] came to him" (1:1, NASB). In fact, on five occasions in this book, Zechariah will affirm that the word of the Lord came to him (1:1, 7; 4:8; 7:1, 8).

In the first message which Zechariah delivered, God called for repentance on the part of Zechariah's audience. Zechariah reminded his contemporaries that although God had been angry with their forefathers, he called them to repentance.

Sometimes people think that anger is incompatible with love—certainly with a God who is love (1 John 4:16). The Scriptures, however, inform us that God does become angry. Anger that arises because the loved one is pursuing a course of action which is ultimately harmful and detrimental is an appropriate form of anger. In fact, the opposite of love is not anger, or even hate. The opposite of love is indifference that does not act for the welfare and benefit of the one loved.

Zechariah then applied the message directly to his audience. He exhorted his countrymen not to be like their forefathers (1:4). The fathers had repeatedly spurned God's injunctions that they return to Him. With what sounds like the lament of a broken-hearted father, grieved by the actions of a beloved child, the Lord reported the outcome of His repeated invitations to return: "But they would not listen or give heed to Me" (1:4, NASB).

The fathers had ignored God's call for repentance; but, through Zechariah, God asked: "Where are they now?" Zechariah reminded his audience that when God speaks, it is not an idle word. God is faithful to fulfill every promise and commitment He makes, whether to discipline or to bless—a fact which Zechariah's audience was called upon to acknowledge (1:6).

This first message delivered by Zechariah reminds us of an important lesson. We can either

How often has the statement "they did not listen or give heed to Me" been God's evaluation of our lives? How often have we done what we wanted, when we wanted, because it was what we wanted regardless of what God's Word might say to us?

listen and heed what God's Word says to us, or we can choose to ignore God and His instructions and face the inevitable consequences.

■ *God exhorted Zechariah's audience not to*
■ *follow in the examples of stubbornness and*
■ *rebellion of their fathers but, instead, to*
■ *repent of their sins and to return to Him.*

SECOND MESSAGE: EIGHT VISIONS (1:7–6:8)

The second message is actually a series of eight visions which Zechariah experienced. Repeatedly Zechariah used phrases such as "I saw," "I lifted up my eyes and looked," or "he showed me" to introduce these visions. Each of the visions involved an angelic messenger to communicate the word of the Lord to Zechariah. Although an angel is not explicitly mentioned in the sixth vision (5:1–4), the unidentified speaker addressing Zechariah certainly seems to be an angelic being, for he spoke for the Lord of hosts (5:4).

In recounting the visions, Zechariah moved rapidly from one to the other. There is often little, if any, transition between the visions.

Once again Zechariah provided a specific chronological marker for his ministry (1:7). Three months after his first message, on the twenty-fourth day of the eleventh month in the second year of Darius, the word of the Lord came again to Zechariah. This message, therefore, dates from the month Shebat (January-February) in the year 520 B.C.

First Vision: The Four Horsemen (1:8–17)

In a vision during the night Zechariah saw a man on a red horse among some myrtle trees in a ravine. Behind the man were three more horses with riders. When he inquired concerning the significance of what he saw, Zechariah was informed that the ones whom he saw had been sent by the Lord to patrol the earth. These riders reported to the angel that they had completed their mission and that the earth was peaceful and quiet (1:11).

The angel of the Lord then addressed the Lord of hosts with a question (1:12). The angel actually voiced the question that had occupied the exiles throughout their time of separation from their land. Despite assurances from prophets such as Jeremiah (see Jer. 29:10–14), the people lamented their plight and wondered when God would have compassion and restore them to their land. In response to the angel's question, God answered with kind and comforting words (1:13). He promised not only to return to Jerusalem, but also to do so with compassion. He promised that His house would be rebuilt and that He would again bring prosperity to His people and their land (1:16–17).

Jeremiah had prophesied that his people would be in exile in Babylonia for a period of seventy years, after which God would restore them and judge Babylonia for its cruelty (Jer. 29:10–14; 25:11–14).

Jealousy among humans is usually an ugly, destructive attitude. How is it, then, that God can describe Himself as "exceedingly jealous" for Jerusalem and Zion? For God to be jealous conveys the sense of His intense commitment to His people and His unfaltering desire for their single-hearted allegiance to Him. God will brook no rival in the affections and loyalty of His people. The Ten Commandments begin with this principle: "You shall have no other gods before Me" (Exod. 20:3, NASB).

The term "Zion" was used in the Old Testament frequently to refer to the city of Jerusalem. The term also was used as a reference to the land of Judah, to the inhabitants of Jerusalem, or to the Israelites, God's chosen people, in general.

In the Old Testament the word *horn* frequently conveyed the meaning of "strength" or "power." The power might refer to that of a nation or kingdom or even the power of a deity. The power of kingship was often symbolized by the term *horn*. For various uses of the word *horn* suggesting "power," see, for example, Jeremiah 48:25; Psalms 75:10; 132:17.

- ■ *In a vision Zechariah heard God speak*
- ■ *words of comfort and encouragement con-*
- ■ *cerning His compassion and concern for His*
- ■ *chosen people.*

Second Vision: The Four Horns and Four Craftsmen (1:18–21)

In his second vision Zechariah saw four horns. In response to his questions concerning what these horns represented, an angel informed Zechariah that they were the nations, or perhaps the leaders of the nations, which had scattered Judah, Israel, and Jerusalem (1:18–19). Zechariah was also shown four craftsmen (1:20). He was informed that the four craftsmen were coming in order to terrify and to overthrow the nations represented by the four horns. The nations which had asserted themselves against Judah would be overthrown and judged by God (1:21).

Since only two nations (Assyria and Babylonia) had scattered Judah, Israel, and Jerusalem by the time of Zechariah, the mention of four horns is somewhat perplexing. The nation of Israel, consisting of ten of the twelve tribes of Israel, had been scattered in exile by the nation of Assyria in 722 B.C. Judah and Jerusalem were scattered by the Babylonians through three deportations. The first occurred in 605 B.C.; the second, in 597 B.C.; and the final deportation took place in 586 B.C., when Jerusalem fell and the Temple was destroyed.

IN

- God assured His people that He had not
- abandoned them and that He would judge the
- nations which had terrified them. The
- nations which had demoralized and domi-
- nated Judah and Israel would themselves be
- terrified and rendered powerless (1:21).

Third Vision: The Man with a Measuring Line (2:1–13)

In his third vision Zechariah saw a man, later identified as an angel (2:3), tasked with measuring the dimensions of Jerusalem. Zechariah was informed that one day Jerusalem would be so prosperous and so full of inhabitants that the population would not be contained by walls (2:4). In fact, in that day, Jerusalem would not need walls for safety and security because the Lord Himself would be a wall of fire around the city (2:5).

For this vision to be accomplished, God would have to call His people home from the widespread dispersion they had experienced at the hands of the Assyrians and the Babylonians (2:6–7). God assured Zechariah and his countrymen of their special place in His love: they were the apple of His eye (2:8). He would judge the nations that had oppressed and afflicted Israel and Judah (2:8–9).

If there were any doubt concerning the proper response to this news, God removed it by instructing His people to sing for joy, to be glad (2:10). The day was coming when God would dwell in their midst; other nations would come to the Lord and would become His people, and Jerusalem and Judah would enjoy the blessings

27

of being His chosen possession (2:11–12). After having just commanded His people to sing for joy and be glad, God commanded all flesh to be silent (2:13). God was about to vindicate His people, and the occasion was one of such awe and solemnity that the proper response of all people on the face of the earth should be awe-filled silence.

- *The third vision indicated that God would*
- *one day bless Jerusalem beyond measure*
- *because His chosen people were the apple of*
- *His eye.*

Fourth Vision: Satan Rebuked; the Branch Promised (3:1–10)

The scene which confronted Zechariah in the fourth vision appears to be a judicial scene set in heaven. Zechariah saw Joshua, the high priest, along with Satan, standing before the angel of the Lord (3:1). The appearance of Joshua was not a pretty one. He was clothed in filthy garments, which the angel commanded to be replaced with festal robes (3:4). Zechariah interrupted the scene in heaven with a request that, in addition to the new clothes, Joshua also receive a clean turban for his head (3:5).

The rebuke of Satan by the angel of God has a parallel in the New Testament. Jude 9 refers to an event not recorded in the canonical Scriptures. Jude informs us that Michael, the archangel, in a dispute with Satan over the body of Moses, rebuked Satan with the words: "The Lord rebuke you!" (NIV).

In verses 8–10 the vision looked to the future. God informed Joshua that He would bring in

By standing at the right hand of Joshua and accusing him, Satan was fulfilling the meaning of his name. The name *Satan* comes into English from the Hebrew word *hassatan*, which means "the adversary," or "the accuser." The New Testament also presents this enemy of God and of His people as the one who accuses and opposes. In Rev. 12:9–10, for example, he is referred to as "the devil" (the Greek *diabolos* means "slanderer") and "Satan" (the Greek *satan* comes from the Hebrew and means "the adversary").

Job 1–2 presents a similar scene with Satan appearing before God in the context of a heavenly council.

His servant, the Branch; that He had set a stone with seven eyes before Joshua; and that He would engrave an inscription on the stone and remove the iniquity of the land in one day (3:8–9). As a consequence of what God promised to do in that future day, everyone would invite his neighbor to sit with him under a vine and under a fig tree (3:10).

To sit under one's vine or fig tree was terminology that recalled the glory days of peace, security, and blessing during the reign of King Solomon (see 1 Kings 4:25). This terminology also was associated with the coming of the Messiah when each person would sit under his vine and under his fig tree (see Micah 4:3–4; John 1:48–50).

The announcement concerning God's servant, the Branch, is often understood to refer to the coming of the Messiah, Jesus Christ. No one knows for certain to what the stone with seven eyes refers; guesses have ranged widely. Some scholars have noted that the Hebrew word translated "eyes" could also be rendered as "fountains" or "springs." If this were the case, then the stone could perhaps be more easily related to the Messiah since Paul, in 1 Corinthians 10:4, identified the stone which provided drink for the Israelites in the wilderness as Christ. If the stone, therefore, is a reference to the Messiah, then the seven "fountains" might suggest the concept of cleansing that would occur in that day when the Lord removed the iniquity of the land in one day.

The designation "the Branch" to refer to the Messiah is found in other Old Testament texts. In a passage understood to refer to the Messiah, Isaiah referred to a branch that would stem from Jesse (the father of King David) on whom the Spirit of the Lord would rest (Isa. 11:1–2). Again, the Suffering Servant song in Isaiah 53 referred to the Servant as one like a tender shoot (Isa. 53:2). According to Jeremiah 23:5, God promised to raise up for David a righteous Branch (same Hebrew word used in Zech. 3:8) who would reign as king. With words similar to those found in Zechariah 3:8–10, Jeremiah also recorded that, in the days of this Branch, Judah and Israel would be saved and would dwell securely (Jer. 23:6). The name of this Branch will be "the Lord our righteousness" (Jer. 23:6; see also Jer. 33:14–16).

29

Zerubbabel was the civil leader of the inhabitants of Judah following their return from the Exile (Hag. 1:1).

■ *Zechariah saw Satan rebuked by the angel of*
■ *the Lord, heard Joshua promised a place of*
■ *service contingent upon his obedience, and*
■ *heard the messianic promise concerning*
■ *God's servant, the Branch.*

Fifth Vision: The Lampstand of Gold and Two Olive Trees (4:1–14)

In the fifth vision Zechariah saw a golden lampstand and two olive trees, one on each side of the lampstand. An angel explained that the lampstand and the olive trees represented the word of the Lord to Zerubbabel (4:6). God wanted Zerubbabel to know that the task for which he was responsible, the rebuilding of the Temple, would not be accomplished through the expenditure of human effort, no matter how mighty or powerful. Rather, the project would be accomplished through dependence upon the Spirit of the Lord of hosts (4:6).

The apparent success and prosperity of individuals who lie, steal, and ignore God's standards for life has often perplexed and troubled God's people. The psalmist, for example, expressed his frustration and consternation as he observed the wicked flourishing, while the righteous struggled and suffered (Ps. 73).

To make this point clear and to encourage Zerubbabel in the task, God addressed a mountain as an obstacle in the path of Zerubbabel (4:7). This mountain would be reduced to a plain before Zerubbabel. In other words, as verse 9 makes clear, the reconstruction of the Temple might be beset with obstacles and difficulties, but because of the presence and provision of the Spirit of the Lord, the project would be completed under Zerubbabel's leadership.

The opposition to the building of the Temple, described as a mountain in 4:7, might refer to that of the enemies living in the vicinity who had done their best to hinder the construction (Ezra 4:1–16). On the other hand, the opposition might refer to the despondency and discouragement of the inhabitants of Judah themselves as they despised the pitifully small beginning of the Temple reconstruction (Hag. 2:3; Zech. 4:10).

Sixth Vision: The Flying Scroll (5:1–4)

Zechariah lifted up his eyes to witness a flying scroll approximately thirty feet long and fifteen feet wide. The scroll represented a curse that was going out upon the people of the land (5:3). The land would be cleansed of those people who stole and swore.

A cubit (v. 2) was a unit of measurement. Technically it was the length measured from the elbow to the tip of the middle finger. The cubit, therefore, typically was considered to be approximately eighteen inches long.

Since swearing itself was not prohibited for the Israelites (see Deut. 6:13; 10:20), the reference to swearing must be to false, insincere oaths made in the name of the Lord. This interpretation is made certain by the words recorded in verse 4, where Zechariah learned that the curse would enter the house of the thief and the one who swears falsely by God's name.

■ *God promised that those who stole and*
■ *swore falsely would receive judgment and*
■ *that His land would be cleansed from such*
■ *wickedness.*

Seventh Vision: The Ephah and the Women (5:5–11)

At the command to lift up his eyes and see, Zechariah observed an ephah in which a woman was sitting. The woman in the basket was identified as "Wickedness," and she was restrained in the basket by a lead covering (5:6–7). Zechariah again lifted up his eyes, and this time he witnessed two women with wings who were carrying the ephah in the air (5:9).

An ephah was a unit of measurement for grain and was approximately one-half bushel. Consequently, the ephah which Zechariah saw was a container slightly larger than a familiar half-bushel basket. (For additional information concerning weights and measurements, see the articles, "Ephah," and "Weights and Measures," in the *Holman Bible Dictionary*.)

The ephah was being carried to the land of Shinar so a house could be built for it there (5:11). Once the structure was finished, the woman, Wickedness (or the ephah containing the woman), would be installed in its place on a pedestal.

The land of Shinar (5:11) cannot be positively identified. The evidence suggests that Shinar was a designation for the region of Mesopotamia. For example, Babel (or Babylon) was located in the land of Shinar (Gen. 10:10).

■ *God promised that wickedness would be*
■ *removed from His people and from their*
■ *land.*

Eighth Vision: The Four Chariots (6:1–8)

Zechariah next observed four chariots emerge from between two bronze mountains. His attention was focused upon the chariots and the distinctive horses pulling them. An angel informed Zechariah that the chariots represented the four spirits of heaven who stood before the Lord of all the earth (6:5). The imagery of four spirits may suggest that these emissaries covered the entire earth, that is, the four corners of the earth.

Apparently, the charioteers accomplished their missions—although only the one to the north country was explicitly mentioned: they caused God's Spirit to rest (6:8). The meaning is probably that as a result of the successful completion of the mission, God's Spirit no longer would strive with the inhabitants of the north. His wrath had been allayed.

The prophets remind us that God specifically promised to judge the land to the north, Assyria and Babylonia, for the severe cruelty inflicted upon Israel and Judah (Zech. 1:21; Jer. 25:12–14; see especially Isa. 14).

One can hardly read the account of Zechariah's eighth vision without thinking of the so-called "four horsemen of the apocalypse" (Rev. 6:1–8). John's vision entailed a white horse, a red horse, a black horse, and a pale or ashen-colored horse. These horses carried out the judgments of God on the earth associated with the first four of the seven seals which were broken. In a similar fashion, Zechariah saw the four chariots with different colored horses carrying out the judgments of God upon the peoples of the earth.

■ *By sending out the four chariots into the*
■ *earth, God appeased His wrath upon the*
■ *inhabitants of the land to the north.*

THIRD MESSAGE: ONE NAMED BRANCH WILL BUILD THE TEMPLE OF THE LORD (6:9–15)

For the first time since chapter one (1:7), the word of God came to Zechariah without being in the form of a vision. He was instructed to collect silver and gold in order to make a crown, and then to deliver a message to Joshua, the high priest. After crowning Joshua, Zechariah was to identify him as the man whose name was Branch, the man who would build the Temple of the Lord (6:12). Of course, in 3:8, we have already encountered a reference to "My servant the Branch." Now this appellation is applied to

The Bible records many promises made by God. Sometimes the promises have an explicit condition stated, as in Zechariah 6:15. Sometimes no explicit condition is stated. Almost always, however, there is an implicit condition underlying God's promises: obedience to His will.

Joshua as the instrument God would use to complete the construction of His Temple.

Somewhat surprisingly, Zechariah referred to Joshua as ruling from his throne and as a priest sitting on His throne (6:13). Since the function of a monarch was to rule and the function of a priest was to serve, one might expect that there would be a conflict between the two offices in one person. Instead of a conflict of interests between the priestly office and the royal office, however, Zechariah indicated that there would be harmony between the two (6:13).

The crown which Zechariah placed upon the head of Joshua was to be a reminder that the Temple would be constructed (6:14). The only condition was that there be complete obedience on the part of the people to what God had commanded them (6:15).

The words of God delivered to Joshua seem to anticipate the ministry of Jesus, the Messiah, who claimed to be a king (see Matt. 21:4–5; John 18:37) and who was, at the same time, our high priest (Heb. 4:14). Furthermore, as a result of the ministry of Jesus, a Temple for God's dwelling has been built which was not constructed by human hands, namely, the body of Christ, the church (Acts 7:48; 1 Cor. 3:16).

- *God promised that the Temple would be built*
- *by a man named Branch. This man would*
- *occupy two offices: priest and king.*

FOURTH MESSAGE: REBUKE FOR SELF-CENTEREDNESS OF THE PEOPLE (7:1–7)

The word of God came to Zechariah in the fourth year of King Darius, on the fourth day of the month Chislev (7:1), that is, 518 B.C. Chislev corresponds to November-December in our calender. The citizens of Bethel inquired concerning whether they should continue to observe the time of fasting and mourning in the fifth month (Ab, July-August) as they had for many years. Although they had inquired of the priests, Zechariah responded to their question with a word from God.

By means of three questions, God informed them that their fasting and mourning in the fifth and seventh months had never been performed for His benefit, but had actually been a self-serving practice of the people for themselves. The reference to fasting and mourning in the fifth and seventh months for a period of seventy years (7:5) referred to the practice of the exiles to grieve and to fast during these months in commemoration of significant catastrophes associated with the Babylonian invasion and domination of their land.

We learn from Zechariah 8:19 that the Jewish people actually observed fasts in the fourth, fifth, seventh, and tenth months as commemoration of events associated with the destruction of Jerusalem, the Temple, and the deportation of the people to Babylonia.

What were the specific catastrophes commemorated by these fasts? On the ninth day of the fourth month, Tammuz, a fast was proclaimed to commemorate the conquest of Jerusalem by Nebuchadnezzar in the eleventh year of Zedekiah (Jer. 39:2; 52:6–7). On the tenth day of Ab, the fifth month, they fasted in remembrance of the destruction of Jerusalem and the Temple in the nineteenth year of Nebuchadnezzar (see Jer. 52:12–13). Jewish tradition tells us that on the third day of the seventh month, Tishri, a fast was observed to remember the murder of

The number of fasts observed by the inhabitants of Judah in the day of Zechariah was notable. The Mosaic legislation prescribed that the people fast on only one day in the entire year, the Day of Atonement (see Lev. 16:29; 23:27–28). Clearly, the exiles had gone well beyond the stipulations of the Law of Moses in their observances of fasts.

Gedaliah, the Jewish governor, and the people who had been left behind in the land following the deportation to Babylon (see 2 Kings 25:25–26; Jer. 41:1). Finally, a fast was kept on the tenth day of the tenth month, Tebeth, because it was on that day that the siege of Jerusalem by Nebuchadnezzar began in the ninth year of Zedekiah (2 Kings 25:1; Jer. 39:1).

- *God rebuked His people for their self-cen-*
- *tered religious observances performed for*
- *their own benefit.*

FIFTH MESSAGE: INSTRUCTIONS AND A REMINDER (7:8–14)

The inquiry concerning fasting prompted the fifth message delivered by Zechariah. He reminded his countrymen of the messages given by the former prophets (7:7, 12). God did not desire for His people to fast in order to get Him to do their bidding. He wanted His people to live lives characterized by justice, kindness, and compassion. Zechariah reminded the people that God was concerned for the powerless and the ignored members of society: the widow, the orphan, the stranger, and the poor—and so should His people be (7:9–10).

Because the forefathers had refused to listen to the messages of the former prophets, they had experienced God's judgment (7:12). Furthermore, as they had treated God, so God returned the favor. They had ignored God and had refused to listen to Him (7:13). Therefore, when they cried out in distress, God refused to listen to them. Instead of listening to His disobedient people, God scattered them and desolated their land (7:14).

The summary of the teaching of the former prophets which Zechariah provides (7:9–10) is very similar to what Isaiah preached concerning the fast which pleases the Lord. According to Isaiah 58:3–12, the fast which is pleasing to the Lord involves abstaining from self-centered self-interests and, instead, practicing justice, kindness, and compassion for others—especially for the most helpless and powerless of society. It is this kind of fast that will move God to bless, not the abstaining from food and drink.

■ *God instructed His people concerning the*
■ *conduct He expected from them and*
■ *reminded them to avoid the practices of those*
■ *to whom the former prophets had been sent.*

SIXTH MESSAGE: PROMISE OF PEACE AND PROSPERITY (8:1–17)

After a reminder of God's displeasure with them for their past refusal to listen and to obey, the sixth message must have come as a welcomed change. In this message God reminded His people of His concern for their welfare. He informed them that He was exceedingly jealous for them and that He would once again favor Jerusalem with the blessing of His presence and fellowship (8:1–3). When this occurred, Jerusalem would be known as the City of Truth, and the mountain of the Lord of hosts would be called the Holy Mountain (8:3).

With God's providential care and blessing, with His presence and fellowship, Jerusalem would one day be populated with people who would

When the Lord of hosts warned His people not to devise evil in their hearts against one another (7:9), He pinpointed a significant cause of the problems that often exist in our society. In fact, the role of one's inner self as the basis for sin and wickedness is a frequently occurring theme in the Scriptures. The writer of Proverbs cautioned, "Watch over your heart with all diligence, for from it flow the springs of life" (Prov. 4:23, NASB). Jeremiah diagnosed the malaise of humanity when he observed, "The heart is more deceitful than all else and is desperately sick; who can understand it?" (Jer. 17:9, NASB). Jesus, likewise, taught that it is out of the heart that evil thoughts, fornications, thefts, murders, adulteries, deeds of coveting and wickedness, deceit, sensuality, envy, slander, pride, and foolishness proceed (Mark 7:21–23).

enjoy the benefits of a faithful relationship with Him (8:4–5). To the audience of Zechariah, such a message probably seemed difficult to fathom. As they contemplated their rather unimpressive numbers and humble achievements, the inhabitants of Judah probably experienced considerable difficulty in visualizing such a day. Consequently, God reminded them that though it might be difficult for them to attain to the promised future, it certainly was not too difficult for Him to accomplish (8:6).

The word of the Lord recorded in 8:9–13 is bracketed by God's exhortation, "Let your hands be strong" (8:9, 13). Because God had promised His favor and protection to the inhabitants of Judah, they were encouraged to look to the future with confidence and a commitment to complete the construction of the Temple. In fact, one of the reasons why they could anticipate the future with assurance was that they were described as "you who now hear these words" (8:9).

This description contrasted strikingly with the description of their forebears, who refused to pay attention, turned a stubborn shoulder, stopped their ears from hearing, and made their hearts like flint (7:11–12). As a result of their obedience, God would reverse the condition of His people. He would not treat them as He had in the former days (8:11). God would now make the land fruitful and productive (8:12). They would now experience God's deliverance and blessing.

Furthermore, God informed His people that He would save them so that they might become a blessing to others (8:13). Consequently, the Lord strongly exhorted His people

If God could exhort His people in the day of Zechariah to let their hands be strong in the light of His promised presence and blessings, how much more encouragement should Christians have today to let their hands be strong and to become a blessing to others. In fact, Christians are promised the permanent indwelling presence of God's Spirit (John 14:16; 2 Tim. 1:14). God Himself promises that it is He who is at work in the believer both to will and to do His good pleasure (Phil. 2:13).

not to fear but to let their hands be strong in the accomplishment of the task to which He had called them.

As God's people, living in covenantal relationship with Him so as to become a blessing (8:13), the inhabitants of Judah and Jerusalem had corresponding responsibilities. God specifically named four areas of conduct for His people to observe: two to practice, two to avoid. They were to practice speaking the truth to one another and rendering sound and true judgments (8:16). On the negative side of the ledger, they were not to devise evil against one another or to love false oaths, since God hated these behaviors (8:17).

In his letter to the Ephesians, Paul used the language of Zechariah 8:16 to exhort his readers to lay aside falsehood and to speak the truth to one another (Eph. 4:25).

Today in the United States many people seem intent upon seeking their own welfare and security, no matter what the cost to others. In fact, even within Christian circles, we often adopt the schemes and tactics of the world in trying to get ahead or to achieve our goals. Have we been guilty of devising evil in our hearts against one another?

- *God promised deliverance, peace, and pros-*
- *perity to His people. He required His people*
- *to let their hands be strong in obedience to*
- *what He charged them to do.*

SEVENTH MESSAGE: GOD'S PROMISED BLESSING UPON JERUSALEM (8:18–23)

Again the word of God came to Zechariah in the form of encouragement and assurance for the inhabitants of Judah. God announced that the four annual fasts, which the people had been observing with grief and mourning, would be turned into feasts of joy and gladness (8:19). In fact, God promised that His own people would be so blessed by Him that many other nations would recognize His favor and would seek to associate themselves with the Jewish people in order to find God and His blessings (8:20–23).

N

- God announced that fasts of mourning would
- be changed into feasts of joy and gladness
- due to His favor and blessings resting upon
- the inhabitants of Jerusalem. So apparent
- would be God's gracious treatment of the
- Jewish people that other nations would seek
- them out in order to find God.

BURDEN CONCERNING THE LAND OF HADRACH AND HAMATH (9:1–17)

Chapter 9 begins a new section in Zechariah's prophetic book. In chapter 9, and again in chapter 12, Zechariah delivered a burden, or oracle, against specific nations. The phrase "the burden of the word of the Lord" did not occur in the first eight chapters, but it is used twice in chapters 9–14. In chapter 9 the burden was directed against Hadrach and Hamath, whereas in chapter 12 the burden was delivered against Israel.

The Hebrew word translated as "burden" or "oracle" in 9:1 is a technical term used in the Old Testament to introduce the oracle of a prophet (see Isa. 13:1; 14:28; 15:1; 17:1; 19:1; Ezek. 12:10; Nah. 1:1; Hab. 1:1; Zech. 9:1; 12:1; Mal. 1:1). The word emphasized that the message of the prophet was something laid upon him for him to deliver to others.

Chapters 9–14 are also distinct from chapters 1–8 in that there are no visions; no angelic messengers appear; no reference is made to rebuilding the Temple; and no mention is made of Zerubbabel and Joshua, two of the primary characters in the book. At this point in the book, Zechariah changed the direction of his prophetic vision, and now his view included nations bordering Israel. God had a word for these nations as well as for His own land of Israel.

Two more characteristics of chapters 9–14 will catch the eye of a careful reader. First, several of the New Testament authors relied upon these chapters for information which they used in their own writings. The following chart shows the distribution of references or allusions to Zechariah in the New Testament.

REFERENCE IN ZECHARIAH	OCCURRENCES IN NEW TESTAMENT
8:16	Ephesians 4:25
9:9	Matthew 21:5; John 12:15
11:12–13	Matthew 27:9–10
12:10	John 19:37
13:7	Matthew 26:31; Mark 14:27

The authors of the Gospels detected several specific references to the Messiah in Zechariah's prophecy. They regarded these prophetic references to be fulfilled in the life of Jesus:

- His triumphal entry into Jerusalem (Matt. 21:5; John 12:15);

- the reference to the crucified Christ as the one who had been pierced (John 19:37);
- the prediction by Jesus on the night He was betrayed that He would be struck and His sheep scattered (Matt. 26:31; Mark 14:27).

This use of chapters 9–14 by the authors of the New Testament suggests that Zechariah was looking beyond the immediate historical situation of his day to events associated with the life, ministry, and death of Jesus Christ. This is not to suggest that Zechariah ceased to address specific historical situations and circumstances in his own day. Rather, the implication is that the prophetic messages referred to more than just the events and conditions existing in the day of the prophet. The lack of any references in chapters 9–14 to Zerubbabel, Joshua, Darius, or to other historical persons, as well as the absence of specific historical circumstances so common in chapters 1–8, supports this view.

A second notable characteristic of chapters 9–14 is the frequent reliance of Zechariah upon prophetic works which predated him. Zechariah apparently made use of Amos 1:9–10 and Amos 5:27–62 in 9:1–8; Jeremiah 25:34–38 in 11:1–3; and Ezekiel 38–48 in 14:1–4. A large portion of chapters 9–14 seems to be Zechariah's interpretation and application of earlier prophetic works.

God's Judgment upon Pagan Nations (9:1–7)

The burden or oracle of the word of the Lord which Zechariah delivered was directed against the lands of Hadrach and Hamath (9:1–2).

Tyre and Sidon (9:2–4) were cities in Phoenicia, a nation on the Mediterranean Sea located just to the northwest of Israel. Although they had

Hadrach cannot be positively identified, but it might be a veiled reference to the Persian Empire. Hamath, which the NIV renders as "Damascus," seems to be associated with Syria, a land to the north of Israel.

been wise to build fortresses and to accumulate riches, their efforts would prove futile because the Lord would overthrow them and consume them (9:3–4). The cities of Ashkelon, Gaza, Ekron, and Ashdod belonged to Philistia, a nation on the southwest border of Israel (9:5–6). These cities, the pride of the Philistines, would be devastated by God (9:5–7).

■ *God pronounced a burden of judgment upon*
■ *Israel's neighbors.*

God's Protection of His People (9:8–10)

In the midst of the oracle directed against Syria, Phoenicia, and Philistia, Zechariah had a word of comfort for the people of Judah. God promised to protect His house (9:8) and to insure that peace would come to His people (9:10). This peace would not arrive, however, independent of the king who would come to Jerusalem, humble and mounted on a donkey (9:9). In a surprising reversal of expectations, Zechariah portrayed the arrival of this king, not mounted on a charging war horse, but entering the city of Jerusalem on a lowly beast of burden. The arrival of Jerusalem's king would be cause for great rejoicing, according to Zechariah, for He would be endowed with salvation for His people, and His dominion would extend over all the earth (9:9–10).

Both Matthew and John cited Zechariah 9:9 in their accounts of Jesus' triumphal entrance into Jerusalem on Palm Sunday (see Matt. 21:5; John 12:15).

■ *In contrast to the judgment pronounced upon*
■ *Israel's neighbors, God promised His people*
■ *a king whose worldwide reign would inaugu-*
■ *rate peace.*

God's Promise of Deliverance (9:11–17)

In a sudden change from the words of peace and salvation associated with the coming king, God spoke of warfare and the deliverance of prisoners. Because of the covenant which He had made with His people, God promised that they would not remain as prisoners in desolate conditions (9:11). In fact, they could have hope because He had committed Himself not only to deliver them but also to restore double to them (9:12).

In 9:13–17 God used the imagery of war against Greece to describe the deliverance of His people. He would use Judah as His weapon against Greece and would fight on behalf of His people so they would conquer. Although the people themselves would fight, it was God who would save them in that day of victory (9:15–16). Instead of being prisoners in desolation, they would experience blessings and prosperity when God delivered them (9:17).

The words recorded in Zechariah 9:13–17 bring to mind the Maccabean period in Jewish history. From 198 B.C. until 167 B.C. the land of Judah was under the domination of the Seleucids. The Seleucids received Syria and Persia when, upon his death, the empire of Alexander the Great was divided among his generals. The reign of Antiochus Epiphanes, one of the Seleucid kings, stands as one of the most notorious periods in Jewish history. Antiochus attempted to compel the Jewish people to abandon their culture and traditions and to embrace Hellenism (i.e., Greek culture, philosophy, and way of life). Among his many attempts to hellenize the Jewish people, he made the practice of the Jewish religion illegal and required the worship of the Greek god, Zeus.

In 167 B.C., Antiochus Epiphanes desecrated the Jewish Temple in Jerusalem by using the altar to offer sacrifices to Zeus. This infamous event eventually led to the Maccabean revolt against the Seleucid dynasty. The Jewish people, under the leadership of the Maccabees, overthrew the domination of the Syrians and became an independent nation in 142 B.C. The time of the Maccabees, therefore, is looked upon as a glorious period in Jewish history.

■ *Because of the covenant which God had with*
■ *Israel, He would not abandon His people to*
■ *suffer in desolation. God Himself promised to*
■ *fight on behalf of His people.*

GOD'S PROVISION AND PROTECTION OF HIS PEOPLE (10:1–12)

Once again God turned His attention to His own people. Initially, He expressed His displeasure with the leaders who had not faithfully or adequately fulfilled their responsibilities (10:1–3). Then God described how He would care for and treat His chosen people (10:4–12).

Condemnation of Inept Shepherds (10:1–3)

God instructed His people to ask Him directly for the spring rains which were necessary for the production of their crops. The people were instructed to approach God with this request because those who had been appointed as leaders, the shepherds of the people, had proven false and inept in the performance of their duties. They had lied to the people and offered false hope and comfort. The result was that the people wandered like sheep and were afflicted. Combining tender imagery and frightening severity, God announced that He had visited His flock, the house of Judah, and, in His anger, would punish the leaders who had proven so ineffective as shepherds of the flock.

■ *God's wrath was provoked by the inept and*
■ *unfaithful service of those appointed to shep-*
■ *herd His people.*

Promise of God's Provision and Protection (10:4–12)

Since the shepherds had failed in their appointed responsibilities, God Himself would act to shepherd His people. Instead of the dishonor and affliction which it had experienced, the flock of God would be strengthened and exalted. God would have compassion upon His people, would save them, would bring them back to their land and into fellowship with Him, and would answer them (10:5–6).

Ephraim, another designation for Israel or for the people of God, would be glad and would rejoice in the Lord as a result of God's intervention (10:7–8). Although the people would be scattered, God promised to bring them back and to cause them to prosper (10:9–10). The nations which had afflicted Israel and Judah would be rendered impotent, while God's flock would be strengthened and would walk in fellowship with Him (10:11–12). This message surely must have brought encouragement and expectant hope to the recipients.

■ *Since the appointed shepherds of God's peo-*
■ *ple had failed in their responsibilities, God*
■ *announced that He would shepherd His peo-*
■ *ple and care for them.*

CONDEMNATION OF LEBANON AND INHABITANTS OF THE LAND (11:1–14)

God commanded Lebanon to receive the judgment prepared for it. God informed Lebanon of its judgment by announcing the destruction of its cedars. What was once a glorious land, full of pride, would be reduced to ruin.

Lebanon was a nation located just north of Israel and was famous for its cedar trees (see, for example, Ezra 3:7; Ps. 92:12). In fact, it was from Lebanon that Solomon imported cedar for the construction of the first Temple (1 Kings 7:2).

In what has to be one of the most difficult passages in the book of Zechariah, the prophet described the people of the land by using the motif of a flock of sheep at the mercy of abusive, self-interested owners and shepherds. Initially, God instructed the prophet to pasture the flock destined for slaughter (11:4). God described those who bought and sold the flock as those who did so only out of greed and self-aggrandizement. There was no concern for the welfare of the flock itself (11:5).

In verse 6 God explained the imagery used in verses 4–5. The flock consigned to slaughter represented the inhabitants of the land of Judah. God foretold a day when He would no longer have pity on the inhabitants of the land. Instead, He would cause the people to be subjugated by powerful kings from whose domination God would refuse to deliver. Exactly when this would occur, or to which precise historical circumstances this message applied, is impossible to identify with certainty.

In response to God's instructions, Zechariah pastured the flock doomed to slaughter, that is, he cared for and protected the inhabitants of the land (11:7). He also made for himself two staffs and named them "Favor" and "Union" (11:7). Not only did Zechariah take over the care of the flock, but he also removed in one month three inept shepherds (11:8). In a surprising turn of events, Zechariah repudiated his responsibility as a caring and wise shepherd and announced that he would no longer pasture the flock (11:9). In fact, he seemed to consign the flock to the announced slaughter by washing his hands of the entire matter and abandoning the flock to its own ineffectual protection.

Matthew reports that Judas Iscariot negotiated a price of thirty pieces of silver for the betrayal of Jesus (Matt. 26:15). Judas returned the silver to the chief priests and elders after he learned that Jesus had been condemned to die. Matthew considered the subsequent use of this money to buy the potter's field to be the fulfillment of Old Testament prophecy. Instead of Zechariah, however, whom he seems to quote, Matthew appeals to Jeremiah as the source of the prophecy (see Matt. 27:9–10). Apparently Matthew saw the conflation of several Old Testament prophecies fulfilled in the actions of Judas and the religious authorities. Nowhere in Zechariah is there any mention of the thirty pieces of silver being used to purchase a field, whereas Jeremiah was instructed to buy a field (Jer. 32:6–9). Nowhere in Jeremiah is there any mention of thirty pieces of silver associated with a potter, whereas Zechariah was directed to throw the money to the potter in the house of the Lord (Zech. 11:13).

As part of his resignation from the office of shepherd, Zechariah cut into pieces the staff named Favor (11:10). This action symbolized the breaking of the covenant he had made with the nations. Just exactly which covenant was broken is not clear in this passage. Had Zechariah made an agreement with the peoples, or was this a reference to a covenant between God and the peoples? Whichever covenant was meant, Zechariah indicated that the oppressed of the flock saw what he did and understood that what they witnessed was a message from God (11:11).

In what seems a remarkable display of chutzpa, after having abandoned the flock and relegating the sheep to certain destruction, Zechariah requested payment for his services as a shepherd (11:12). He apparently did not care whether he was paid, or how much he received. The flock, or perhaps the owners of the flock, paid Zechariah thirty pieces of silver for his wages as the shepherd.

Based upon the words of God recorded in verse 13, the reader learns that the thirty pieces of silver were, in actuality, the valuation that the people placed upon God as their shepherd. With taunting words of sarcasm concerning the magnificent sum, Zechariah was instructed to take the silver and throw it to the potter in the Temple. At this point in the narrative Zechariah cut his second staff, Union, into pieces, thus severing the brotherhood between Judah and Israel (11:14).

■ *God, by describing Zechariah as a shepherd*
■ *who abandoned the sheep, described the refusal*
■ *of His people to accept Him as their Shepherd.*

CONDEMNATION OF THE WORTHLESS SHEPHERD (11:15–17)

Because He was going to raise up a foolish, inept, self-indulgent shepherd over the flock, God instructed Zechariah, in a symbolic gesture, to take again the equipment of a foolish shepherd (11:15–16). Although this shepherd would arise at the initiative of God Himself, God pronounced a woeful judgment upon him (11:17). This foolish shepherd would decimate the flock through his self-indulgent indifference and neglect, but he would receive severe injury as a result of his abandonment of the flock.

Of course, the union between Israel and Judah, technically, had been severed following the death of King Solomon when ten tribes had united, under Jeroboam, to form the Northern Kingdom of Israel and two tribes had remained loyal to Rehoboam, the son of Solomon, to constitute the Southern Kingdom of Judah (see 1 Kings 12).

- God announced that He would use an inept
- leader of Israel to accomplish His purposes,
- and then He would judge the inept shepherd
- for the folly inflicted on Israel.

BURDEN CONCERNING ISRAEL (12:1–14:21)

Beginning in chapter 12, Zechariah delivered an oracle concerning Israel. This message occupied the prophet's attention throughout the last three chapters of the book. A frequently recurring phrase in this portion of Zechariah's prophecy was "in that day." The phrase only occurs four times in the first eleven chapters; it occurs seventeen times in the last three chapters. The frequency of the occurrence of this term is a key to the significance of these last three chapters. God was announcing significant events which would occur in the future, "in that day." The phrase "in that day" therefore, was an eschatological reference. It referred to a time associated with the end of the age or the inauguration of God's kingdom into this age.

One element of the preaching of Jesus was that the kingdom of God was at hand (Matt. 4:17; 9:35; 10:7; 12:28; Mark 1:15; Luke 17:21).

Protection of Judah Promised (12:1–9)

God began this oracle concerning Israel with a rather elaborate introduction of Himself, emphasizing His creative and sovereign activities (12:1). He is the one to whom all of creation belongs because He is the one who brought it all into existence.

The Lord announced that a day was coming when Jerusalem and Judah would be confronted by enemies. In that day, God would make Jerusalem so powerfully effective that the nations surrounding it would suffer (12:2–3) and would experience divinely inflicted confusion and dismay (12:4–5). In that day the house of David, through whom the Messiah would come (see 2 Sam. 7:12–16), would be such an effective leader that it would serve as the angel of the Lord to protect and to defend the nation from its enemies (12:7–9).

In his account of the crucifixion of Jesus, John referred to the prophecy recorded in Zechariah 12:10. John regarded the crucifixion, along with the soldier's piercing of the side of Jesus with a spear, to be a fulfillment of these words of Zechariah (John 19:37). Although John did not cite the words of Zechariah concerning the mourning and weeping as for a firstborn son, a reader familiar with the New Testament can hardly avoid seeing their applicability to Jesus and His crucifixion.

■ *Although a day was coming when Israel*
■ *would be confronted by its enemies, God*
■ *announced that He would equip His people*
■ *with power so they would overcome their foes.*

Prediction of Mourning for Jerusalem (12:10–14)

God promised to pour out on the house of David and the inhabitants of Jerusalem a spirit of grace and supplication (12:10). The inhabitants would then look on the one they had pierced—God Himself (12:10). As a result, the people would weep and mourn bitterly as would be the case when a firstborn son, an only child, dies (12:11–12).

- When the house of David and the inhabitants
- of Jerusalem pierced God, as they certainly
- would, they would each experience inconsol-
- able grief and mourning.

Promise of Cleansing from Sin and Impurity (13:1–6)

In the day of national mourning over the one who had been pierced, God promised to act to cleanse the land of sin, impurity, idolatry, false prophets, and the unclean spirits which had polluted the land and the people. In a somewhat surprising use of terminology, similar to that used to describe what had happened to God, Zechariah declared that, in that day, the false prophet would be pierced by his own father and mother (cp. Zech. 12:10 and 13:3). In that day, those who attempted to prophesy would be ashamed and would disclaim being a prophet at all (13:4–6).

- In the day that God acted to cleanse His land
- of all impurity and unrighteousness, no one
- would want to pronounce a false prophecy.

Salvation of a Remnant (13:7–9)

Suddenly Zechariah's message took a dramatic turn. The Lord of hosts called for a sword to awake and to spring into action against someone identified as "My Shepherd," "My Associate" (13:7, NASB). God commanded that the Shepherd be struck so that the sheep might be scattered. God would turn His own hand against the little ones.

Both Matthew and Mark recorded that Jesus, on the way to the Garden of Gethsemane on the night He was betrayed, informed His disciples that they would all fall away that night because of Him (see Matt. 26:31; Mark 14:27). Jesus indicated that this would occur because it was written, "I will strike down the Shepherd, and the sheep shall be scattered," a direct quotation of Zechariah 13:7 (NASB). Consequently, the reference to God calling for a sword to strike His Shepherd so that the sheep might be scattered found its fulfillment in the betrayal and arrest of Jesus, the Good Shepherd, and the desertion of Him by His disciples, the sheep of His flock.

Although the Shepherd would be struck and the sheep scattered, God announced that He would preserve a remnant of His people (13:8). This remnant would be refined and purified as though subjected to the refiner's fire (13:9). God identified this faithful remnant as His people, and they would address Him as "my God" (13:9).

The reader familiar with the use of Zechariah 13:7 by Jesus to refer to Himself (Matt. 26:31; Mark 14:27) can hardly read this passage without recalling that, although the majority of the Jewish nation rejected their Good Shepherd, there were some who did respond in faith to Him and who ultimately remained faithful—although they were scattered and refined through persecution and trials. Once again, therefore, the reader is reminded that Zechariah had his eye on the future and was describing events which would occur "in that day" when God acted to cleanse and purge the land (13:1–2) and to pour out upon His people the spirit of grace and supplication (12:10).

- God promised that He would preserve a
- faithful remnant of His people through the
- purification process which awaited them.

Promise of Future Deliverance (14:1–8)

Although chapter 14 begins with what sounds like promising news, the report quickly turns quite dismal. Zechariah announced that a day was coming when God would gather nations against Jerusalem and that the city would be devastated with half of its inhabitants carried off into exile (14:1–2). Even in the midst of such bad news, however, there was good news. The day was coming when God Himself would fight against those nations which had afflicted Jerusalem and His people (14:3).

As a matter of fact, "in that day" there would be some remarkable topographical occurrences in the land of Judah. God would stand on the Mount of Olives and the mount would be split in two by a valley running from east to west (14:4). Through this valley the inhabitants of Jerusalem would flee from the city (14:5). Associated with this event, Zechariah announced that God, "my God," would then come, accompanied by His holy ones (14:5). This day, known only to God, would be a unique day because there would be neither daytime nor nighttime.

- Using dramatic language, God promised to
- intervene in history to deliver His people
- from their enemies.

Security of Jerusalem Promised (14:9–11)

In the day of God's battle against the nations which had ravaged Jerusalem, God would be acknowledged as king over all the earth (14:9). With the exception of Jerusalem, the land would be turned into a plain from Geba (located a few miles north of Jerusalem in the territory of Benjamin) to Rimmon south of the city (14:10). Jerusalem itself would remain on Mount Zion and the people would live in it securely without any curse upon them or their city (14:11).

The proper interpretation of Zechariah 14:1–8 has been much debated. Some see this as a prophecy which will be fulfilled when Jesus returns with His saints (usually referred to as the rapture; see 1 Thess. 4:13–17) and literally stands on the Mount of Olives—with all of the associated topographical upheavals. Others prefer to see the language in a more symbolic sense to describe the ultimate victory of God over the forces of evil and the vindication of His kingdom and His people. Regardless of how one interprets the details of this passage, the final result is essentially the same: God acts in behalf of His people and for their ultimate blessing.

- When God delivered His people, He would be
- acknowledged as the king over all the earth.
- There no longer would be a curse associated
- with Jerusalem.

Judgment on the Enemies of Jerusalem (14:12–15)

In exceptionally grotesque language, Zechariah described the plague of judgment which God would inflict on all those who had gone to war with Jerusalem (14:12). In that day God would send a great panic upon these enemies of His people, and they would be thrown into a state of confusion and turmoil and would turn against one another (14:13).

- God promised to devastate completely all those
- who had opposed and oppressed Jerusalem.

Ultimate Exaltation of Jerusalem (14:16–21)

If any of those who had waged war against God's people survived the plague described in 14:12–15, and the events associated with "that day," they would go to Jerusalem to worship God and to celebrate the Feast of Tabernacles (14:16). In fact, any nation or people which did not celebrate the Feast of Tabernacles, or who refused to submit to God's reign, would be deprived of rain (14:17–19). Of particular significance in this passage is the announcement that all the peoples of the earth would worship God. There would no longer be any distinction based upon nationality or ethnic origin. What would be significant was not one's nationality or race, but whether one worshiped God, the King.

"In that day" even the most common of objects (cooking utensils) and beings (horses) would be considered holy to the Lord (14:20–21). Through such imagery Zechariah indicated that Jerusalem and its people would be completely committed to and dedicated to God. The impurity and sin which had contaminated the land had been removed (13:1–2); God had delivered His people and triumphed over His foes (14:1–15), and the land now was "holy to the Lord." Zechariah indicated that the distinction between the sacred and the profane, between the clean and the unclean, had been eradicated because there no longer remained anything profane or unclean. Everything was now considered sacred and clean—holy to the Lord.

For something to be regarded as holy to the Lord meant that it was dedicated and set apart for the Lord's service and use. This same terminology was used, for example, to refer to the high priest on whose turban were inscribed the words, "Holy to the LORD" (Exod. 28:36–38). The Sabbath was holy to the Lord because it was a day set apart and dedicated to God. In fact, anything set apart for the sole use of God was referred to as "holy to the LORD" (see Lev. 27:28).

The Feast of Booths, also known as the Feast of Tabernacles or the Feast of Ingathering, commemorated the years when the Israelites had wandered in the wilderness under the leadership of Moses. During this period of wilderness wandering, the Hebrews had lived in temporary shelters or booths. The week-long observance began on the fifteenth day of Tishri (October-November) and was a reminder of God's protection and preservation of His people. For injunctions concerning the observance of the Feast of Tabernacles, see Leviticus 23:33–36, 39–44 and Deuteronomy 16:13–15.

QUESTIONS TO GUIDE YOUR STUDY

1. Can God's people continually ignore with impunity God's calls to repent? (1:1–6)

2. Can a God of love also express anger toward His people? (1:2)

When Zechariah stated that there would no longer be a Canaanite in the house of the Lord (14:21), he referred to the fact that God's judgment had purified the people and the land and had removed all that was impure and unholy. The term *Canaanite* represented the people whom God had expelled from the Promised Land, a sinful people who had exhausted God's mercy and reaped His judgment (Lev. 18:24–30; Deut. 7:1–11; 9:4–5).

3. What was the primary message communicated by God to the audience of Zechariah by means of the eight visions? (1:7–6:8)

4. Whom does God describe as the apple of His eye? (2:8)

5. Who was identified as the Branch and what was his ministry to be? (3:8–10; 6:11–13)

6. If God's people refuse to listen when He calls, what does God promise to do in response? (7:13)

7. Do you think the audience which received the messages delivered by Zechariah went away encouraged and hopeful or discouraged and fearful of the future?

8. Which passages in Zechariah did the authors of the Gospels apply to the life and ministry of Jesus? (9:9; 11:12–13; 12:10; 13:7)

9. To what does Zechariah refer by use of the phrase "in that day"? (chaps. 12–14)

10. When the book of Zechariah concludes, what is the status of God's people? (14:20–21)

MALACHI

INTRODUCTION

As the twelfth and final book among the minor prophets, Malachi is the last book in the Old Testament section of the English Bible. It also occupies the final position among the minor prophets in the Hebrew Scriptures.

The text of Malachi consists of several indictments which God brought against His people. These indictments are in a dialogical form. God pronounced an accusation against His people; they then responded by asking how the indictment could be true or on what basis God could make such an assertion against them. To the questions posed by His people, God responded with the basis of His accusation. In all, the book of Malachi contains twenty-six questions: thirteen posed by God to His people and thirteen by the people to God.

No definitive statements are found in the book of Malachi concerning the date when the prophet ministered. However, based upon similarities in the conditions reported among the people, and the status of the worship practices associated with the Temple in Jerusalem, the prophet Malachi seems to have been a contemporary of Ezra and Nehemiah. For example, Malachi functioned after the Temple had been rebuilt in Jerusalem following the return from the Babylonian Exile. The fact that Malachi accused the people of a lackadaisical attitude toward the sacrifices suggests that the sacrificial system had been operating for some time prior to the prophet's ministry (see Mal. 1:7–14). The priests had also grown complacent and indifferent in their service toward God (Mal. 2:1–9;

The name *Malachi*, means "my messenger" or "my angel."

Neh. 13:27–30). Furthermore, Malachi had to address a widespread disregard for marriage vows and rampant divorce (Mal. 2:14–16). Apparently, like Nehemiah, Malachi had to contend against the practice of marriage with women from foreign nations and the concomitant unfaithfulness to God produced by such unions (cp. Mal. 2:10–16 with Neh. 13:23–29). The people in the time of Malachi were also guilty of not paying the required tithes (Mal. 3:8–12; see also Neh. 13:10–13). If Malachi was a contemporary of Nehemiah (445–415 B.C.), which seems most likely, then his ministry would have occurred some time around the last two or three decades of the fifth century B.C.

INTRODUCTION (1:1)

The book of Malachi begins with an introduction describing the contents of its message and identifying both the recipients of the message and the agent who conveyed the message. As did Zechariah (Zech. 9:1; 12:1), Malachi introduced his message as a "burden" or "oracle" of the Word of God.

God's message, delivered through Malachi, was addressed to Israel. Israel, technically, was the name of the Northern Kingdom, composed of ten tribes, during the time of the divided monarchy. The name was also used in the Old Testament to refer to the Jewish people, in general, as God's people. The book of Malachi, therefore, is a record of the burden of God's word to His people delivered through His messenger, Malachi.

FIRST INDICTMENT: ISRAEL QUESTIONS GOD'S LOVE (1:2–5)

The first indictment God brought against His people involved His love for them and their failure to recognize that love. God began by declaring His love for His people (1:2). To this declaration of love, Israel demanded to know how God had demonstrated His love. God answered by reminding the Israelites of His loving choice of their ancestor Jacob while rejecting Jacob's brother, Esau.

The love/hate language used by God to describe His choice of Jacob and His rejection of Esau should be understood as covenantal, election language. God instructed the Israelites themselves that they were not to despise the descendants of Esau (see Deut. 23:7–8). Would God absolutely hate those whom Israel was commanded to permit to enter the assembly of the Lord after the third generation (Deut. 23:8)? To love Jacob and to hate Esau essentially meant that God chose Jacob to fulfill the promises made to his grandfather Abraham, while Esau was not the object of the same electing love.

The Israelites should have recognized God's love for them because they knew that He loved the father of the twelve tribes of Israel and chose to fulfill His covenantal promises through him. With the covenant made to Abraham, and reiterated to Jacob (Gen. 28:13–15; 35:10–12), also came the responsibility of obedience to the stipulations of the covenant. Israel's failure to keep its covenantal obligations often resulted in failure to enjoy the expected blessings. During such times, the Israelites frequently questioned God's love for them—as they did in the day of Malachi.

Edom was not the object of God's covenantal love and, therefore, had no basis to expect God's blessings and prosperity (1:3–4). This did not keep Edom from doing everything in its power to achieve material success and prosperity. In

Is it possible that Christians today might fall into the error of Edom? Might we decide what we want to accomplish in our own personal lives, or even in the life of our church or ministry, without determining what God wants to accomplish? As the psalmist reminds us: "Unless the Lord builds the house, they labor in vain who build it" (Ps. 127:1, NASB).

Esau, and the descendants of Esau, constituted the nation of Edom (Gen. 25:30; 36:1, 8, 9).

fact, in the face of calamity, Edom courageously rebuilt and refused to accept defeat. What Edom did not understand, however, was that God had committed Himself to oppose their prosperity, and all their efforts would ultimately prove futile. God promised the Israelites that they would see the demise of Edom and would then praise Him for His covenant-keeping love (1:4–5).

■ *Despite Israel's doubts concerning His love,*
■ *God affirmed that He loved His people. His*
■ *choice of Jacob over Esau, demonstrated by*
■ *His opposition to Edom's prosperity, proved*
■ *His love for Israel.*

SECOND INDICTMENT: PRIESTS DISHONOR GOD (1:6–2:9)

The indictment of the priests comprises the longest section in the book of Malachi. This section is notable for the harshness and severity of Malachi's denunciation of the priesthood.

In the Old Testament, only Malachi uses the term "the LORD's table" (1:7) to refer to the altar upon which the sacrifices were presented.

The indictment of the priesthood begins with two questions based upon analogies drawn from household relationships. God compared Himself to a father or to a master in a home (1:6). Any father, or slave master, received honor from his son and from his slaves. God charged the priests of Israel with withholding the honor due Him and of despising His name. When the priests demanded to know how they had despised His name, God informed them that they had done so by presenting unworthy sacrifices to Him (1:7). In fact, the conduct of the priests was so manifestly improper that God asked them whether the governor of the land

According to the Mosaic legislation, only unblemished sacrifices were acceptable to God (Lev. 22:18–25). If an animal had any defect, it was not to be presented to the Lord as an offering.

would condone such spiteful and disrespectful treatment (1:8). The priests knew full well that if they treated the governor the way they treated God, they would not be received kindly, nor would they have any expectation of having their petitions granted. Consequently, they should have understood that they had no expectation of having their entreaties granted by God (1:9).

God was so displeased with the priesthood that He expressed the desire that the gates to the Temple might be shut so as to prevent further unworthy and defiled sacrifices (1:10). In blunt and direct language, God informed the priests that He was not pleased with them and that He would not accept an offering from them (1:10). In a remarkable reversal of what one would expect, God informed the priests that His name would be treated with respect and honor among the nations, even while it was being treated with contempt and dishonor by the very priests who had received His revelation and stood in a special relationship to Him (1:11–14).

Apparently familiarity and the daily routine had produced contempt on the part of the priesthood. They considered their service to God as tiresome and somehow beneath them (1:13). God, however, announced to this disdainful priesthood that He was a great King and that He would not tolerate being treated in this shameful and disgraceful manner (1:14).

With solemn and sobering words God issued a commandment to the priests of Israel (2:1–9). If they did not change their ways and honor Him properly, God would curse them, would spread the garbage of the defiled sacrifices on their faces, and would have them taken away with the trash

Is it possible that Christians might unintentionally develop a contemptuous familiarity with God and the things of God? Can we fall into a routine of church attendance and activities performed by rote and lose sight of the One whom we approach?

from their feasts. God would take these steps, not to abandon His covenant with Levi, but to insure that the covenant might continue and be fulfilled (2:4–5). The priests in Malachi's day were violating the covenant. They had concluded that their special privileges as priests gave them privileged positions with God. They no longer revered God's name or stood in awe of Him.

Priests who functioned in accordance with the intent established in God's covenant with Israel had specific characteristics. A priest faithful to the covenant would fear God, would provide true instruction, would not speak unrighteously, would walk with God in peace and uprightness, would turn many back from iniquity, would preserve knowledge, and would serve as the messenger of the Lord of hosts (2:6–7).

The priests to whom Malachi was sent, however, had turned aside from the way of God. Through their misguided instruction they had caused many others to stumble and had actually corrupted the covenant which God had established with Levi (2:8). Since the priests had despised God and treated Him with contempt and dishonor, God informed them that He had made them despised and abased before all the people (2:9).

God's treatment of the priests of Israel in Malachi's day reminds us of a principle which the New Testament makes explicit: "Do not be deceived, God is not mocked; for whatever a man sows, this he will also reap" (Gal. 6:7, NASB). The priests to whom Malachi was sent thought they could despise the name of the Lord with impunity; but they learned, to their dismay, that they were grievously mistaken. They received in their own lives what they had sown. What does our daily life reveal concerning our attitude toward God?

■ Israel's priests were dishonoring God through
■ their shameful and disdainful service. Unless
■ they changed their ways and honored God in
■ their service, God promised to send a curse
■ upon them. God instructed them concerning
■ what He expected from His priests.

THIRD INDICTMENT: GOD'S PEOPLE DEAL TREACHEROUSLY (2:10–16)

God's third indictment of Israel addressed the manner in which the people treated one another. Although the Israelites were like a family with one father and one God and should have cared for and loved one another, they actually dealt treacherously with one another. Their treatment of one another resulted in the profanation of the covenant which God had made with their ancestors (2:10).

The two questions posed by God, recorded in Malachi 2:10, implied that, by virtue of having one father (either Abraham or, perhaps, God Himself) and one Creator, the Israelites should have been experiencing unity, harmony, and obedience to the wishes and standards of their common father and Creator. Their conduct, however, was incongruous because they were acting treacherously toward one another. They lacked the qualities which should have characterized them: family loyalty, love for one another, obedience to their father's will, and trust toward one another. The Israelites acknowledged the validity of God's interrogation of them when they responded by asking, "Why do we deal treacherously each against his brother?" (2:10, NASB). The Israelites did not dispute the fact of their incongruous conduct; they wanted to know its cause.

Not only had the Israelites dealt treacherously with one another, but they had also dealt treacherously with their God (2:11–12). Behaving as spiritual adulteresses, they had been unfaithful to God. God charged His people with marrying the daughter of a foreign god.

"Marrying the daughter of a foreign god" (2:11) could refer to at least two ideas. First, the Israelites might have married non-Israelites, i.e., people who worshiped false deities. In Numbers 21:29, for example, the Moabites are referred to as "sons and daughters of Chemosh." Based upon the contents of the books of Ezra and Nehemiah (Ezra 9–10; Neh. 13:23–29), we know that this was an issue which plagued Israel during the days of Malachi's ministry. Secondly, the phrase might also refer to idolatry on the part of God's people. The two ideas are related to one another since the Israelites often succumbed to idolatry through marriage with idolaters.

As a result of their unfaithfulness to God, the Israelites had profaned His sanctuary and had committed an abomination in the land. Israelites guilty of such conduct were to be excluded from fellowship with God and from those who had remained faithful to Him (2:12). Such condemned people had deliberately rejected a faithful relationship with their God; consequently, God would cut them off from the tents of Jacob.

The Israelites were aware of God's displeasure and rejection of them due to their unfaithfulness (2:13). They were expressing great distress over the fact that God did not seem to accept their offerings or treat them with favor. Apparently the tears shed by the Israelites were not tears of repentance, but tears of remorse. They were sad because they could not have their cake and eat it too. They wanted to live as they pleased, in unfaithfulness to their God but yet, at the same time, to enjoy God's blessings.

Although they were aware of God's rejection of their offerings, the Israelites professed ignorance concerning the cause of this rejection (2:14). When they inquired concerning the reason for God's displeasure, God informed them that He was taking the witness stand against them to testify that they had behaved treacherously with their wives. Due to the rampant practice of divorce, God indicted the Israelites for violating the covenant of marriage. In fact, using some of the harshest language in the Bible concerning divorce, God declared, "I hate divorce" (2:16).

In a day when divorce has become commonplace, even among Christians, the words of the Lord recorded in Malachi might seem unduly harsh. We need to remember several points, however. The Old Testament certainly

The apostle Paul could speak of a sorrow according to the will of God which leads to repentance and of a worldly sorrow that leads to death (2 Cor. 7:9–10). The Israelites addressed by Malachi apparently were expressing the latter type of sorrow. Might Christians today sometimes be guilty of excessive displays of emotion which mask false piety and unfaithfulness to God? Genuine sorrow according to the will of God leads to repentance. Mere sorrow over the lack of God's blessings may indicate a stubborn, rebellious spirit that resists unreserved loyalty to God alone.

acknowledged the practice of divorce among the Israelites and legislated certain regulations for remarriage after divorce had occurred (see Deut. 24:1–4). Nevertheless, Jesus explained that divorce had been permitted during the Old Testament period due to the hardness of the hearts of the people—hardly an endorsement for divorce (see Matt. 19:4–8; Mark 10:5–9). The teaching of Jesus, later reinforced by Paul, informs us that God's intention for marriage was one man and one woman bound by a covenantal relationship for life (see Matt. 19:3–12; Mark 10:2–12; 1 Cor. 7:1–11). Although we certainly should not relegate the sin of divorce to some special category, as though it were the only sin God hated, neither should we minimize God's expressed hatred of such a sin.

Is it possible, with regard to the matter of divorce and remarriage, that Christians today have been influenced more by the culture in which we live than by the teaching of our Lord?

■ *God indicted the Israelites for their unfaith-*
■ *ful and treacherous conduct toward Him,*
■ *toward one another, and toward their*
■ *spouses.*

FOURTH INDICTMENT: ISRAEL PERVERTS RIGHT AND WRONG (2:17)

The indictment levied against Israel which begins at 2:17 may well continue until 3:15. The fourth indictment, stated in 2:17, accused the Israelites of perverting good and evil by virtue of their attitudes toward God. Then, in 3:13–15, God again charged the Israelites with uttering arrogant words which perverted good and evil. These two accusations, addressing the speech of the Israelites and their attitudes as expressed by their words, may serve to bracket this unit within Malachi. Nevertheless, for the sake of clarity and emphasis, each indictment in the section 2:17–3:15 will be considered separately in the presentation which follows.

When Malachi charged the Israelites with wearying God with their words, they demanded to know how they had done so (2:17). God informed them that they had wearied Him by perverting good and evil in at least two ways. First of all, they asserted that those who practiced evil were actually good and the objects of God's favor. In the second place, they accused God of moral indifference by suggesting that He really was not concerned with justice and what constituted right and wrong. Both of these accusations maligned the character of God: not only did He allow evil people to prosper, but He approved of their conduct—God had gone to sleep on the job and had failed to execute justice.

Through Malachi, God informed the Israelites that He was tired of such speech on their part. They had not exhausted God by the quantity of their words; they had exasperated Him by the quality of their words.

■ *God indicted the Israelites for their perver-*
■ *sion of good and evil. They called evil good*
■ *and accused God of culpable indifference*
■ *concerning justice.*

PROMISE CONCERNING THE MESSENGER OF THE COVENANT (3:1–7)

God did not allow the challenge regarding His character and His reputation to go unanswered. The Israelites had accused God of regarding evil to be good and of not showing up to execute justice. Therefore, God informed the Israelites

---

Jesus emphasized the importance of the words which we utter when He taught that what comes out of one's mouth indicates the content of one's heart (Matt. 12:34). In fact, Jesus went on to assert that "every careless word that men shall speak, they shall render account for it in the day of judgment. For by your words you shall be justified, and by your words you shall be condemned" (Matt. 12:36–37, NASB).

that He would appear with judgment and justice, but it would not be what they expected.

God promised to send a messenger to prepare the way before Him (3:1). The identity of this messenger has been debated. Since the term translated "messenger" is actually the Hebrew word *malachi*, some have suggested that the prophet Malachi himself was the messenger sent to prepare for the Lord's imminent arrival. Others have concluded that the reference was to the entire line of Old Testament prophets whom God had sent to Israel. Another suggestion has been that the messenger was the prophet Elijah. This last suggestion has the support of Malachi 4:5–6, in which the Israelites were informed that God would send Elijah before the coming day of the Lord.

According to Malachi 3:1, there seemed to be an element of imminence associated with the appearance of this messenger. He would appear suddenly as the messenger of the covenant to prepare the way for the Lord. In somewhat ironic language, God essentially announced to the Israelites: "You have asked, 'Where is the God of justice?' (2:17). Behold, the One you seek will appear suddenly to execute justice." In fact, when the messenger of the covenant appeared, his ministry would involve purifying and refining the people of Israel. Although his ministry would be so terrifying and so stringent that the people would despair of their ability to endure it, his ministry would be one of cleansing, not destruction. Since Malachi had already indicted the priests for presenting defiled offerings to God (1:6–14), he now indicated that a specific intent of the messenger's ministry would be to purify the sons of Levi so that they might once again present offerings in righteousness (3:3). The

The New Testament provides a helpful interpretation concerning Malachi 3:1, as well as Malachi 4:5–6. Three of the Gospels used Malachi 3:1 to refer to John the Baptist (Matt. 11:10; Mark 1:2; Luke 7:27). When Luke reported the announcement of the birth of John the Baptist by the angel Gabriel, Luke specifically referred to Malachi 3:1 and 4:6 to describe the future ministry of John (Luke 1:16–17). Jesus, when asked to explain why tradition required Elijah to come prior to the day of the Lord, stated that Elijah had, in fact, already come, and that John the Baptist was the one who fulfilled the prophecy in Malachi (Matt. 11:10, 14; 17:10–13; Mark 9:11–13).

consequence of his ministry, therefore, would be a people once again pleasing to God, as in the days of old (3:4).

The Israelites had cast aspersions upon God's character. They had accused Him of fickleness, of not only tolerating evil but also approving of it, and of lacking concern for justice (2:17). Consequently, God informed them that He Himself would come to them to inflict judgment upon evil and to contend for the helpless, that is, to seek justice on behalf of the oppressed (3:5–7). God explicitly declared to the Israelites that "I, the LORD, do not change" (3:6 NASB). Israel had ignored the fact that if it were not for God's unchangeable nature, the nation would have been consumed by God's judgment already. God reminded the people that He remained faithful to His promises and to His covenants with the nation of Israel despite their fickleness and unfaithfulness (3:6–7).

Repeatedly, throughout their history, God had pleaded with His people to depart from their unfaithful ways and to return to Him, but they had consistently turned aside. Even in the day of Malachi, instead of complying with God's warning to return to Him, they inquired concerning how they should return—as though they did not know (3:7).

For God to declare that He does not change (Mal. 3:6) means that He is dependable and trustworthy. He does not change in His character or His nature. Unlike our human associates, God will always be the same; He will not be fickle or subject to whims or prove unreliable. We do not have to fear that God might one day change and be different from what He has been in the past. We can rejoice with the author of the book of Hebrews that "Jesus Christ is the same yesterday and today, yes and forever" (Heb. 13:8, NASB).

- *God promised to send His messenger to*
- *refine and to purify His people and to judge*
- *the unrighteous.*

FIFTH INDICTMENT: ISRAEL ROBS GOD (3:8–12)

In response to Israel's inquiry regarding how the nation might return to God, God informed it that one way to return was to begin obeying the law regarding the tithe. In 3:8–12 God indicted Israel for its lack of obedience in presenting the required tithes and offerings to Him. Consequently, in answer to Israel's question, "How shall we return?" God replied, "By ceasing to rob me through the withholding of the tithes and offerings" (3:8).

For information concerning the obligation of the Israelites with regard to the tithe, consult the following: Leviticus 27:30–33; Numbers 18:21–32; Deuteronomy 12:5–18; 14:22–29; 26:1–14.

God made the shocking announcement that the Israelites were robbing Him (3:8). One immediately wonders how a human being could possibly rob God. Can a human being take from God what belongs to Him or overcome Him so as to steal His possessions? In fact, Israel asked precisely this question: "How have we robbed you?" (3:8). Israel challenged God to present the evidence of their theft. He informed them that the entire nation was robbing Him by withholding the tithes and offerings; and, therefore, they were under a curse (3:9).

In what must have seemed a stunning suggestion to the Israelites, God instructed them to put Him to the test. He proposed a test of His faithfulness. He invited them to bring the required tithes to Him in order to see if the anticipated blessings would not be forthcoming (3:10). In fact, God promised the Israelites that, in response to their obedience, He would cause their blessings to overflow to such an extent that all the nations would acknowledge them as a blessed and delightful land (3:11–12). Of course, this was precisely what God had promised His people: obedience brings blessings and

The curse which the Israelites experienced for their failure to present the tithes and offerings to God probably referred to the curse announced in Deuteronomy 28:15–16: failure to observe all of God's commandments would bring curses upon the people. The curses involved diseases, disasters, crop failures, droughts, and pestilences (Deut. 28:20–25)—precisely the kind of conditions which were being experienced by the Israelites during the ministries of Haggai, Zechariah, and Malachi. Instead of viewing their conditions as God's wake-up call to prompt them to repent of their sins, the Israelites accused God of changing and of going back on His promises of blessing.

disobedience brings cursing (cp. Deut. 28:1–2 with Deut. 28:15).

God promised the Israelites that they would not be able to contain His blessings if they stopped robbing Him and began to bring the whole tithe into His storehouse. Before He would bestow the blessing, however, the people would have to do the very thing they had refused to do: return to Him in repentance and obedience.

Should we interpret Malachi 3:10–11 to teach that if Christians practice tithing, they will experience God's overflowing blessings in the material realm?

We need to remember that the tithe in the Old Testament was legislated in order to meet needs: those of the Levites, widows, orphans, and aliens. Jesus criticized the Pharisees and scribes for tithing while neglecting the more important matters of the law: justice, mercy, and faithfulness (Matt. 23:23). These words of Jesus were not intended to teach that Christians are not required to tithe; rather they were words of rebuke to those living under the old covenant who attempted to earn God's favor through external compliance with certain laws while avoiding the selfless compassion and concern God demanded from those whose hearts belonged to Him. The New Testament principle concerning giving is that Christians should give, based upon what God has provided, generously and cheerfully to meet the needs of others in accordance with God's guidance in each situation (see Luke 6:38; 2 Cor. 8:12; 9:6–7).

Lest we conclude that God's invitation to put Him to the test is a universal principle that applies to all people at all times, we need to note that there are times when God does not encourage or condone human beings putting Him to the test. The psalmist warned against putting God to the test as the Israelites had done during the time of the Exodus (Ps. 95:8–11; see also Num. 14:22–23). Jesus refused to put God to a test when Satan tempted Him to do so by suggesting that He leap from a pinnacle of the Temple on the basis of a scriptural promise taken out of context (Matt. 4:7). To step out in faith when God invites us to test His faithfulness is a matter of obedience. To put God to the test without His invitation is a matter of presumption and sin.

- *God indicted the Israelites for robbing Him*
- *by withholding the presentation of the*
- *required tithes and offerings. He invited them*
- *to test His faithfulness to bless them if they*
- *would bring all the tithes into His store-*
- *house.*

SIXTH INDICTMENT: ISRAEL UTTERS ARROGANT WORDS (3:13–15)

Once again God reminded the Israelites that they had expressed arrogant, harsh, strong words against Him (3:13). The Israelites demanded to know what they had spoken against their God which had aroused His ire. The answer was not long in coming, for God proclaimed that His people had announced that it was futile to serve Him (3.14). On what basis had the Israelites reached this conclusion? They had observed that they were not experiencing the blessings of Deuteronomy 28 as they had anticipated. Apparently, they had concluded that they had faithfully served God for nothing. Of course, the Israelites remained insensitive to the fact that each of God's indictments, pronounced through Malachi, was intended to convict them of their failure to keep His charge and to walk obediently before Him. The hardheartedness of the Israelites had progressed to the point that they were blind to their own spiritual condition, but they once again accused God of indifferently allowing the wicked to prosper and to escape judgment (3:15).

To select arbitrarily a ten percent tithe as the maximum level of giving required of Christians would be to miss the significance of the teaching of the New Testament. Christians are to give compassionately to meet needs without consulting their calculators or the IRS code. We are to consult God who will provide guidance in each situation to the humble believer who waits to do His will.

To seek God only for His blessings, or what He can give us, seems to be a continual temptation for God's people. Even our evangelism often invites people to try Jesus so that their lives will be enhanced or so that they will experience greater self-fulfillment. God certainly promises blessings and rewards to those who serve Him, but our motivation for serving Him should be for His glory and not for our material prosperity.

- *God indicted the Israelites for their harsh,*
- *arrogant, and strong words spoken against*
- *Him. Despite their claims to the contrary,*
- *God charged the Israelites with not serving*
- *Him and not keeping His charge.*

GOD'S MESSAGE OF REASSURANCE (3:16–4:3)

Reassurance to Those Who Fear God (3:16–17)

Malachi indicated that there were some Israelites who feared the Lord and who paid attention to the messages which he delivered (3:16). Malachi also indicated that God paid attention to those who paid attention to Him. A book of remembrance was written before God for those who reverenced and esteemed His name. The book of remembrance served as a reminder to God of those individuals who were faithful to Him and who would be spared when He visited His people in judgment (3:17). Those who feared the Lord and who esteemed His name truly constituted God's own special possession. Those whom God numbered as His own special possession served Him with the loyalty and respect of a lovingly obedient son, not with the grudgingly external compliance of a constrained prisoner.

Only in Malachi 3:16 does the phrase "scroll of remembrance" occur in the Old Testament. There are other references in the Old Testament, however, to a book in which God recorded the names of His people (Exod. 32:32–33; Pss. 69:28; 87:6; Dan. 12:1).

- *Those who feared God and lived in obedience*
- *to Him were declared to be God's own special*
- *possession. They would be recorded in God's*
- *book of remembrance.*

A Day of Vindication and Judgment Promised (3:18–4:3)

Although the Israelites in the day of Malachi had been indicted by God for their failure to distinguish between good and evil (2:17; 3:15), Malachi prophesied that the day was coming when the people would once again distinguish between the righteous and the wicked (3:18). The distinction between those who truly served God and those who did not would become clear because, in the day of God's visitation, He would judge the unrighteous with the consuming fire of His wrath (4:1). Those who feared the name of God, however, would experience the healing warmth of His love and would prosper and overcome the wicked (4:2–3).

- *God promised a day in the future in which*
- *the wicked would be burned up in the fire of*
- *His judgment while the righteous would*
- *experience the healing warmth of His love.*

EXHORTATION TO REMEMBER THE LAW OF MOSES (4:4)

As the book of Malachi concludes, God instructed the Israelites to remember the law of Moses, His servant. God reminded Malachi's audience that the law given to Moses at Horeb was for all Israel—which included them. To remember God and His law was not merely a mental recollection; to remember God meant that one feared and esteemed His name by living obediently by His statutes and ordinances. Those who would live in this manner would be recorded in God's book of remembrance.

The conclusion of Malachi with its reference to a curse stands in stark contrast to the final chapter in Zechariah with its prediction that "there will no more be curse" (Zech. 14:11, NASB).

Matthew relied upon Malachi 4:5 to refer to John the Baptist and his ministry (Matt. 11:14; 17:10–13). The angel Gabriel informed John's father that his son's ministry would involve turning many sons of Israel back to their God (Luke 1:16).

Since the last word in the book of Malachi is the word *ban*—which could be translated as "curse" or "anathema"—the Masoretic text, the traditional Hebrew text, directs the reader to repeat verse 5 after reading verse 6 in order to avoid such a harsh conclusion to the book. Actually, in the Hebrew text there is no fourth chapter. The Hebrew text regards 4:1–6 in the English text as the concluding verses of chapter three, i.e., 3:19–24.

■ *God commanded Israel to remember the law*
■ *which He had given the people through His*
■ *servant Moses.*

PROMISE CONCERNING THE APPEARANCE OF ELIJAH (4:5–6)

As the recorded prophecy of Malachi came to a close, God promised that He would send the prophet Elijah to His people before the great and terrible day of the Lord (4:5). The ministry of Elijah would be to restore familial love and respect, to turn the hearts of the children to their parents and the hearts of the parents to their children (4:6). The purpose of Elijah's ministry was so that God would not come and strike the land with a curse.

■ *God promised that He would send Elijah to*
■ *His people to prepare them prior to the great*
■ *and terrible day of the Lord.*

QUESTIONS TO GUIDE YOUR STUDY

1. When God desired to prove His love for the Israelites, to what did He direct their attention? (1:2–5)
2. In what way were the Levitical priests dishonoring God through their service in the Temple? (1:6–14)
3. Based upon what God said to the Levitical priests, is it true that any religious service is better than no religious service? (see 1:10)
4. What qualities characterize a Levitical priest who serves God genuinely? (2:4–7)

5. How does God describe the marriage relationship and His attitude toward divorce? (2:13–16)

6. What will be the purpose of the messenger whom God promises to send to Israel and what will be his ministry? (3:1–6)

7. If God could declare that He does not change, could He also assert that Israel had not changed either? (3:5–7)

8. How had Israel robbed God? (3:8–9)

9. In what way and for what purpose did God invite Israel to put Him to the test? (3:10–12)

10. How had Israel spoken arrogant or harsh words against God? (3:13–15)

11. What did God promise for those who feared Him and who esteemed His name? (3:16–17)

12. What did God promise the wicked in the day which was coming? (3:18–4:3)

13. Whom did God promise to send to Israel and what was his ministry to accomplish? (4:5–6)

The following is a collection of Broadman & Holman published reference sources used for this work. They are provided here to meet the reader's need for more specific information and/or for an expanded treatment of the books of Haggai, Zechariah, and Malachi. All of these works will greatly aid the reader's study, teaching, and presentation of the books of Haggai, Zechariah, and Malachi. The accompanying annotations can be helpful in guiding the reader to the proper resources.

Cate, Robert L. *An Introduction to the Old Testament and Its Study*. An introductory work presenting background information, issues related to interpretation, and summaries of each book of the Old Testament.

Dockery, David S., Kenneth A. Mathews, and Robert B. Sloan. *Foundations for Biblical Interpretation: A Complete Library of Tools and Resources*. A comprehensive introduction to matters relating to the composition and interpretation of the entire Bible. This work includes a discussion of the geographical, historical, cultural, religious, and political backgrounds of the Bible.

Farris, T. V. *Mighty to Save: A Study in Old Testament Soteriology*. A wonderful evaluation of many Old Testament passages that teach about salvation. This work makes a conscious attempt to apply Old Testament teachings to the Christian life.

Francisco, Clyde T. *Introducing the Old Testament*. Revised Edition. An introductory guide to each of the books of the Old Testament. This work includes a discussion on how to interpret the Old Testament.

Holman Bible Dictionary. An exhaustive, alphabetically arranged resource of Bible-related subjects. An excellent tool of definitions and other information on people, places, things, and events of the books Haggai, Zechariah, and Malachi.

Holman Bible Handbook. A summary treatment of each book of the Bible that offers outlines, commentary on key themes and sections, illustrations, charts, maps, and full-color photos. This tool also provides an accent on broader theological teachings of the Bible.

Holman Book of Biblical Charts, Maps, and Reconstructions. This easy-to-use work provides numerous color charts on various matters related to Bible content and background, maps of important events, and drawings of objects, buildings, and cities mentioned in the Bible.

Sandy, D. Brent, and Ronald L. Giese, Jr. *Cracking Old Testament Codes: A Guide to Interpreting the Literary Genres of the Old Testament.* This book is designed to make scholarly discussions available to preachers and teachers.

Smith, Ralph L. *Old Testament Theology: Its History, Method, and Message.* A comprehensive treatment of various issues relating to Old Testament theology. Written for university and seminary students, ministers, and advanced lay teachers.

SHEPHERD'S NOTES